The Manawaka World of
MARGARET LAURENCE

The Manawaka World of
MARGARET LAURENCE

Clara Thomas

McCLELLAND AND STEWART LIMITED

Grateful acknowledgement is made to the following for permission to reprint:

Longmans Canada Limited, excerpts from *The Chosen Tongue* by Gerald Moore. **North Texas State,** source material from "The Novels of M. Laurence" from *Studies in the Novel* Vol. IV (Summer 1972) No. 2, pp. 145-164. **Macmillan & Co. Ltd.,** excerpts from *Long Drums and Cannons* by Margaret Laurence; by permission of Macmillan, London and Basingstoke. **Oxford University Press,** excerpts from "The Cracked Mother" from *Islands* by Edward Brathwaite; reprinted by permission of Oxford University Press, Toronto. **Houghton Mifflin Company,** excerpts from *Song of the Lark* by Willa Cather; reprinted by permission of Houghton Mifflin Company, Boston. **WLWE,** source material from "The Short Stories of Margaret Laurence" from *World Literature Written in English,* Group 12, m.l.a. V.11:1, April 1972, pp. 25-34. **Journal of Canadian Fiction,** excerpts from "A Conversation About Literature: An Interview with Margaret Laurence and Irving Layton" Vol. 1, No. 1 (Winter 1972); reprinted by permission. **Heinemann Educational Books Ltd.,** "Beware Soul Brother" and "The Explorer" by Chinua Achebe from *Beware Soul Brother;* reprinted by permission of Heinemann Educational Books Ltd. **Macmillan of Canada,** excerpt from *Fifth Business* by Robertson Davies; reprinted by permission of The Macmillan Company of Canada Limited, Toronto. **Faber and Faber Ltd. & Harcourt Brace Jovanovich, Inc.,** lines from "Little Gidding" from *Collected Poems 1909-1962* by T. S. Eliot, reprinted by permission of Faber and Faber Ltd.; from "Little Gidding" in *Four Quartets* by T. S. Eliot, copyright 1943, by T. S. Eliot; copyright 1971, by Esme Valerie Eliot; reprinted by permission of Harcourt Brace Jovanovich, Inc. **John Ciardi,** excerpts from "On Writing and Bad Writing" by John Ciardi, from *Saturday Review,* December 15, 1962. **McClelland and Stewart Ltd.,** excerpts from *The Prophet's Camel Bell, The Tomorrow-Tamer, This Side Jordan, The Stone Angel, A Jest of God, A Bird in the House, Jason's Quest, The Fire-Dwellers, The Diviners,* and excerpts from "Roblin's Mills (2) by Al Purdy from *Selected Poems;* reprinted by permission of The Canadian Publishers, McClelland and Stewart Limited, Toronto.

Every reasonable care has been taken to trace ownership of copyright material. Information will be welcome which will enable the publisher to rectify any reference or credit.

Contents

To my parents,
and Strathroy,
their town and mine.

Foreword

Margaret Laurence is a Canadian writer, solidly rooted in southwestern Manitoba, the setting of Neepawa, her home town, and of Manawaka, her fictional one. Her characters "talk Canadian"; in their idiom and turns of speech we hear "Canadian" as distinct from "American" English. Moreover, in their dilemmas, her characters move us through four generations of the history of this country, from the western pioneer experience of Jason Currie and Timothy Connor through two world wars and the Depression, to the contemporary setting and problems of Stacey Cameron and Morag Gunn. The powerful impact of her novels in this country, where *The Stone Angel* alone has sold 78,000 copies in the New Canadian Library edition, reflects the identification her readers feel with her themes and her characters.

We risk being too narrowly nationalistic, however, if we define her simply as "Canadian," or even more restrictedly—by region—as a "prairie writer." She is regularly published in England and America as well as in Canada; various of her works have been translated into French, German, Italian, Spanish, Dutch, Norwegian, Danish, and Swedish, and because of *Long Drums and Cannons*, her study of Nigerian novelists and playwrights, she is known and respected among students of African literature everywhere.

In the deepest sense, Margaret Laurence belongs with the most gifted writers of the emergent nations, countries which, like Canada, must find and recognize their own cultures and their own voices. In her convictions about the writer's place in society and in the themes of her fiction, she is particularly linked to Chinua Achebe and Wole Soyinka of Nigeria, and Edward Brathwaite, Derek Walcott, and George Lamming of the West Indies. She would agree with Achebe's strong sense of social mission in a changing, post-colonial world: "The writer cannot be expected to be excused from the task of re-education and regeneration that must be done." She is equally challenged by the demands and the responsibilities of the art and the craft of fiction.

The Manawaka World of Margaret Laurence is a discussion of the progress to date of her writing from the translations of Somali folk tales (*A Tree for Poverty*, 1954) to *The Diviners* (1974), the fifth of her Manawaka works. It incorporates material from my *Margaret Laurence* (1969), in McClelland and Stewart's Canadian Writers Series, as well as from various articles I have written over the past five years.

I am particularly grateful to Doris Brillinger of York University's Secretarial Services for her patience and skill in the typing of this manuscript and its many revisions. Jo-Anne Degabriele and Dorothy Cockburn, also of Secretarial Services, have been unfailingly helpful to me. I am indebted to Margaret Pappert for her intensive work in compiling the Checklist of materials in the Scott Library, York University, and to Bernice Lever for her assistance with the bibliography in its early stages. And I owe thanks to Margaret Laurence herself for information about her family background, for permission to quote extensively from her unpublished lecture, "Gadgetry or Growing? . . Form and Voice in the Novel," and for our many discussions of the art and the craft of fiction.

*The Yoruba symbol of eternal repetition, an
abstract figure of the snake eating its own tail.*

"The tropical forest does not evoke symbolism of a seasonal
death followed after some interval by a seasonal resurrection,
but rather of a continuous, unbroken process of decay and
renewal. Thus the snake's ever-devouring mouth expresses life
drawing its sustenance from decay and death, even as the
young shoots of the forest do."

Gerald Moore, *The Chosen Tongue*

"The dilemma of gods is that however much they may love or
hate mankind, in the end it is men themselves who decide their
own fates, not in any theoretical way, not in a state of vacuum,
but with deep emotional reference to their fathers and their
gods. Maybe at some point our ancestors and our gods will be
free of us. But not quite yet."

Margaret Laurence, *Long Drums and Cannons*

The Simpsons

Above left: Margaret Simpson Wemyss.
Above: Verna Simpson Wemyss.
Left: John Simpson, father of Verna and Margaret, grandfather of Margaret Laurence.

The Wemyss

Top: Great-grandmother Catherine Wemyss, at the time of her marriage to Robert Wemyss.
Left: Grandmother Margaret Harrison Wemyss.
Right: Grandfather John Wemyss.

Left: Margaret Laurence as a baby with her father Robert Wemyss, her grand-mother Wemyss, and great-grandmother Wemyss.
Above: Margaret age two, at Clear Lake, Manitoba.
Below: Margaret with her father and step-mother, Margaret Simpson Wemyss.

Above: Jack and **Margaret**
Laurence in Somaliland.
Right: Margaret, age 17. (The
horsewoman stance is a pose, she
reports. She was always scared of
horses.)
Below: Margaret Laurence with her
children Jocelyn and David.

ONE

The Ancestors

We shall not cease from exploration
And the end of all our exploring
Will be to arrive where we started
And know the place for the first time.

T. S. Eliot *Little Gidding*

Margaret Laurence has created Hagar, Rachel, Stacey, Morag,
and all the other people of her Manawaka world out of a
gigantic complexity, reaching back from her own place and
time through four generations of men and women in a
Canadian western town. All the strands of her ancestral past
have interwoven with her own life and the power of her own
gift impelling her to write her people down, to liberate them
from her imagination to the pages of her fiction. She quoted Al
Purdy's lines,

but they had their being once
and left a place to stand on

as the epigraph to *The Diviners*, and the conviction they
express forms one of the strongest strands in the fabric of her
work. She is intensely conscious of the generations behind
her—and of the constant, random role that chance, especially
death, plays in the lives of men and women. It was chance that
brought her grandfather, John Wemyss, to Neepawa, Man-

itoba, instead of to Aligarh, in the northwestern provinces of India, where he had planned to practise law.

The Wemyss records, letters, diaries, and documents go back to the early nineteenth century, to the marriage of her great-great-grandparents, John Wemyss and Margaret Morrison, at Newhalls Inn, in 1817. The Wemyss' were a Lowland Scotch family, a sept of the Clan MacDuff, with their own plaid pin and the motto, *"Je pense."* They came from Burntisland in Fifeshire (John Wemyss of Neepawa maintained that their name meant "cave-dweller" and that they were descended from the Picts, the aborigines of Scotland).

True to both the necessity and the vocation of the Scottish people in the nineteenth century, they spread out over the globe. One of the sons of John and Margaret was Robert, born in 1824, Margaret Laurence's great-grandfather. He was a tea-merchant in Edinburgh until the 1870's. Then, because of business losses and hopeful of opportunity for his family in a new land, he emigrated to Canada and became a sheep-rancher near Raeburn in Manitoba. There is a very striking resemblance between Margaret Laurence and a photograph of her great-grandmother, Catherine, the lady who moved in middle age from the comfortable life of a well-to-do businessman's wife in Edinburgh to the raw and lonely life of a rancher's wife in the Canadian West.

Another of the sons of John and Margaret became a lawyer and a baronet, Sir John Wemyss of Aligarh in India. When Robert and Catherine came to Canada, they left their son John to matriculate from Glasgow Academy and then to serve his apprenticeship with a legal firm in Glasgow. He was to go into the Indian Civil Service as a lawyer under his Uncle John's sponsorship; in one of the old letters, written in 1877, Sir John holds out both the financial advantages and the glamour of India to his nephew:

> You get £40 per month as an assistant magistrate which gradually rises to £250 when you become a judge maybe 15 to 20 years hence. . . . I have been

away at a celebrated fair . . . we all lived in tents,
there was a Ball every other night and we had capital
fun. I bought a mare for my dog cart, I could not walk
much about the fair as I was a cripple from a fall I had.
I had to ride an elephant.

Wrapped with that particular letter is a black-bordered "In
Memoriam" card, "in Affectionate Remembrance of Sir John
Wemyss, Bart., who died at Aligarh, North West provinces of
India, 8th of March, 1878, aged 47."

John Wemyss' plans were radically changed by his uncle's
death. When he finished his apprenticeship in 1881, he
followed his family to Canada, practising for a time in
Winnipeg and then moving to Neepawa where he incorporated
the town. He married Margaret Harrison, the daughter of Dr.
D. H. Harrison who was briefly the premier of Manitoba when
the Norquay government fell in 1887. This generation's John
and Margaret had three children—Robert (the eldest, born in
1896, who was Margaret Laurence's father), John, and Norma.

Robert Wemyss went to St. Andrew's college in Ontario.
He began articling with the law firm of Mulock in Winnipeg;
then in the First World War he and his brother John joined the
60th Canadian Field Artillery at the same time, as gunner and
driver respectively. They fought in France and they survived.
John Wemyss came back to work for the United Grain
Growers, managing a grain elevator in Wilkie, Saskatchewan,
until his death; Robert returned to finish articling with his
father in Neepawa and then to become a partner in the firm of
Wemyss and Wemyss, Barristers and Solicitors. In 1922,
Robert Wemyss married Verna Simpson of Neepawa, a
talented pianist and music teacher. Their daughter, Jean
Margaret, was born on July 18, 1926.

The Simpson great-grandparents had come from County
Tyrone, Ireland, to Ontario about 1850, bringing with them
their two sons, Joseph and Will. Margaret Laurence's maternal
grandfather, John Simpson, was born near Milton, Ontario, in
1856. When his father died he was twelve, and he left school to
become an apprentice to a cabinet-maker. Then, about 1878,

he went west and took up cabinet-making in Portage La
Prairie. There, in 1886, he married Jane Bailey, whose family
had come to Canada as Loyalists and had emigrated west from
Amherstberg, Ontario. The couple moved to the burgeoning
little town of Neepawa, where John became an undertaker, as
many cabinet-makers did, and ran a furniture store. The
Simpsons had seven children—Stuart, Ruby, John, Rod,
Margaret, Verna, and Velma.

In 1930, at the age of thirty-four, Verna Simpson Wemyss
died suddenly of an acute kidney infection. Her older sister
Margaret, a teacher in Calgary, came home to look after her
four-year-old niece, Margaret Wemyss. A year later she and
Robert Wemyss were married. Their son, Robert, was born in
1933, only two years before his father died of pneumonia. A
few months later, Grandmother Simpson died. In 1938
Margaret Simpson Wemyss, with her two children, moved
into Grandfather Simpson's house to look after him. There the
young Margaret Wemyss lived until she went to United College in 1944. Grandfather Simpson died in 1953 at the age of
ninety-seven.

Margaret Simpson Wemyss was a clever and a loving
woman, a great and continuing influence on the life and work
of Margaret Laurence. Eight years older than her sister,
Verna, she had had a successful and respected teaching career
when she came home to Neepawa in 1930. In fact, as a girl she
had graduated from high school with the highest marks in the
province of Manitoba. According to her father's creed, university was out of the question for a woman, but school teaching was acceptable. She always treasured an inspector's report
of 1922 which commented on her "marked ability" and especially on her teaching of literature—"she seeks to bring out
literary appreciation" in her students.

When she moved into her father's house he was an old
man of eighty-two; her children were five and twelve, and she
was a widow with very little money. The intensity of Margaret
Laurence's imaginative perception of the burdens laid on one
generation by another seeded itself in these years. So did her
empathy with particular women and their need to struggle

towards freedom of the spirit—and so did her own fierce independence of spirit. When she lived in his house, Margaret resented her grandfather's authority over them all. His strength was her constant challenge to battle. She was challenged, but certainly not crippled, by this old, still fierce and autocratic man; her step-mother's supportive love and encouragement and her own strong spirit, well-matched to her grandfather's strength, were constant, counterbalancing dynamics towards growth and achievement.

Margaret Laurence was especially fortunate in Margaret Simpson Wemyss' early recognition and encouragement of her talent. As far back as she can remember she was making up imaginary characters and situations and then, later, writing stories. Her step-mother, who was always "mother" to her, took her work seriously. "She read my work; she encouraged me and she also criticized my work. She was always honest with me about it," says Margaret Laurence, "and so was one of my teachers, Miss Mildred Musgrove." Her mother loved books and had some that Margaret Laurence still treasures—a copy of *Paradise Lost*, for instance, finely, and fittingly, bound in cobra skin, which impressed her deeply in her teens. Margaret Simpson Wemyss was a founder of the Neepawa Public Library, and worked tirelessly and stubbornly to keep it going during the Depression years. And always she shared an enthusiasm which was almost a reverence for literature with her step-daughter.

The events, the circumstances, and the places of her past are particularly important to an understanding of both the "why" and the "what" of Margaret Laurence's writing. She does not confine herself to her own experiences, though many of these she has transmuted into her fictions. But she does always write from within a circumference that contains the imaginative experiences and perceptions congruent with one of her place, her time, and her life—and no others. This strict self-limitation, as it shows itself, for instance, in the outsiders' point-of-view of the *Tomorrow-Tamer* stories, or the limits of Rachel's understanding of Nick in *A Jest of God*, is a part of the consistent integrity of all her work.

The town of Neepawa, its geography, its history, and its community of people as she knew them in the 1930's and early 1940's, have likewise provided a geographical, historical, and social circumference for the place and people of Manawaka. Neepawa is about 125 miles northwest of Winnipeg:

> Situated on a plateau overlooking a valley to the east and south, the land rises northwest of the town to form the south slope of the Riding Mountain, which contains the beautiful Riding Mountain National Park. . . . In the valley to the southeast of Neepawa the Boggy and Stoney Creeks merge to form the White Mud River which empties into Lake Manitoba. . . . Fertile soil extends in all directions from Neepawa, and ever since the time of the first settlers the area has been an important wheat-growing region.
>
> (A. F. McKenzie, *Neepawa, Land of Plenty*, 1958)

Its district was originally settled in the late 1870's by a group of Scottish pioneers, trekking westward from Ontario like the Wemyss' great-grandparents, to take up land in the challenging, promising West. Sixty years earlier, a shipload of the dispossessed and destitute tenants of the Duchess of Sutherland had struggled to reach Alexander Selkirk's land. Many perished on the way, but the survivors reached their goal and founded the Red River colony around the joining of the Red and Assiniboine Rivers, where Winnipeg now stands. Thus the later stream of Ontario-Scottish immigrants merged their particular qualities of mind and spirit with the first strong Scottish backbone of all Manitoba settlement.

Manawaka is not Neepawa, but its geography, the details of its situation, its landmarks, and its people depend on Margaret Laurence's experience of Neepawa and on her ability to store in memory and to transmute what she knew and what she felt of it into a created fictional world. All the history of her town has been woven into the fabric of the Manawaka works, but particularly the cataclysmic events of her own time: the effects of the First World War and the actuality of the Depression and the Second World War. Chance set and predetermined her ancestors and her place of growth; some alchemy of heredity also predetermined her talent. The personal experiences of her childhood, their strong tensions between loss and love, challenge and achievement, had begun a very early forcing and encouraging of that talent in the direction of her mature work. Vanessa MacLeod's two-scribbler novel, *Pillars of the Nation*, was, in fact, a story written by Margaret Laurence when she was twelve, for a Winnipeg *Free Press* contest. The town of Manawaka had already then taken shape in her imagination—her story began this way: "The name of Manawaka comes from Indian words. Their meaning has been buried for so long that it can never be found, not even in the spring ploughing."

It was 1956, however, and she was thirty years old, before Margaret Laurence began to make herself known as a writer—"Drummer of All the World" is the beginning of her professional fiction. Since then, and particularly since 1960, her achievement has been prodigious. There have been five novels: *This Side Jordan* (1960), *The Stone Angel* (1964), *A Jest of God* (1966), *The Fire-Dwellers* (1969), and *The Diviners* (1974); two story-collections: *The Tomorrow-Tamer* (1963), and *A Bird in the House* (1970); and *Jason's Quest* (1970), a children's book. Besides fiction, her translation of Somali folk-tales, *A Tree for Poverty*, was published in 1954, *The Prophet's Camel Bell,* the story of the Laurences' years in Somaliland, in 1963, and *Long Drums and Cannons*, a study of Nigerian fiction, in 1968.

Ever since her first novel, *This Side Jordan*, Margaret Laurence has been published in Canada by McClelland and Stewart. In those early days of her career, Jack McClelland was instrumental in arranging for simultaneous publication with Macmillan in England; later his enthusiasm for her work, and his persistence, achieved its acceptance by the firm of Alfred Knopf in New York; ever since, Margaret Laurence's fiction has been published simultaneously in three countries, by McClelland and Stewart in Canada, by Macmillan in England, and by Alfred Knopf in the United States. Her special place among Canadian writers and the special bonds between her work and Canadian readers have been recognized by a great variety of awards and marks of esteem: in 1960 *This Side Jordan* won the Beta Sigma Phi prize for a first novel by a Canadian; *A Jest of God* was awarded the Governor General's Medal in 1966; in 1961 and 1962 her short stories received the University of Western Ontario President's Medals; in 1967, United College, the University of Winnipeg, made Margaret Laurence an Honorary Fellow, the first woman and the youngest person to be so honoured; McMaster, Dalhousie, Trent, the University of Toronto, and Carleton University have conferred honorary degrees on her, and in 1972 she was made a Companion of the Order of Canada. She is in demand among Canadian universities as a writer-in-residence and has so served at the University of Western Ontario, the University of Toronto, and Trent University.

The honours do credit to Canada's consciousness of Margaret Laurence's talent and of her uniquely Canadian voice. More important, however, is her wide readership in this country and beyond. Her voice, in the persons of Hagar and Rachel, Jules Tonnerre and Christie, Stacey and Morag, is being heard. Like her own concern with the ancestors, her works cross boundaries of time and space. Readers of all ages, of both sexes and many languages respond to her perceptions of the dilemmas that are common to men and women everywhere.

TWO

"Departures I"

The Prophet's Camel Bell;
A Tree For Poverty

We carry within us all the wonders we seek without us
There is all Africa and her prodigies in us.

Sir Thomas Browne

In 1944 Jean Margaret Wemyss left Neepawa with a scholarship to go to United College in Winnipeg. Everyone who knew
her there remembers her as Peggy Wemyss and also
remembers the dynamism of her personality and its double
commitment—to literature and to large and liberal causes.
United College in the forties was an Arts and Theology college
of about 750 students, an affiliate of the University of Manitoba. Its principal was Dr. W. C. Graham and its special pride
was a tradition of independent thought and action, a not-so-
unlikely phoenix to have sprung from its early foundations: the
province's early Methodist seminary, Wesley College, and its
Presbyterian counterpart, Manitoba College. The enthusiasms
of Margaret Wemyss would have blossomed in any college
atmosphere, but the powerfully positive, liberal idealism of
which she was a part at United College exactly complemented
her own intensity, her sympathy for individuals, and her emotional rejection of all social systems that would humiliate men
and women and constrict their freedom.

13

She took honours in English at United College; her developing writing talent has constantly assimilated and made use of this literary training. She has always been a "literary" writer in the pattern of her works and allusions, in her experiments with form and voice, and supremely so in her ability to stand back, to look at her writing, and to describe the processes of its creation with both analytic precision and critical perception. Among her professors, the late R. N. Hallstead was especially important to her; the energy of his enthusiasm about literature, about writing, and about all humane causes, won, lost, or embattled, matched her own. Among the friendships begun in the Winnipeg years, her association with Adele Wiseman, founded on compatibility in talent and temperament, and on the kinship of one who was born to write for another of that ilk, was—and is—strongly supportive.

United College's undergraduate publication, *Vox*, carried several of Margaret Wemyss' literary experiments in various forms and moods: "Calliope," a short story about a little boy lost among carnival side-shows, which was a very early experiment with one of her dominant and recurrent themes—the child threatened by an alien environment; a criticism of the poetry of Robinson Jeffers, remarkable for an acute, unsentimental, and unyielding honesty of vision; a witty little child's poem, and some bad poems with memorable lines. These last are memorable because the body of Margaret Laurence's later writing so strongly substantiates their early statements. A poem beginning "This is the land of living things," ends with these lines:

> Quietly I walk, wind-cloaked,
> Hearing the rain's promise
> That this land will be my immortality.

Again, these romantic, youthful lines from a poem called "Song of the Race of Ulysses" make a bond that Margaret Laurence has kept, central to herself and to all that she has written:

This alone of vagrant thought I know
That if the pines, harped with black thongs of wind,
Should mould a harsh exultant symphony of storm,
I would arise unquestioning and follow.

It is neither convenient hindsight nor overblown romanticism to talk of "a sense of mission" or "a sense of destiny" with regard to the life and work of Margaret Laurence. "I have been writing most of my life," she says, "and always knew that I wanted to be a writer, but did not believe for many years that this was something one could do as a profession." From as far back as she can remember she was *writing* and she *had* to write—groping, learning, discarding, succeeding, but always and above all *practising* the craft of words. Her training in English literature gave her both depth of literary experience and breadth of understanding of the forms and techniques which she would later draw from. As John Ciardi has said,

> The human passion is first, but it must yet be joined by an equal passion for the medium before good writing can happen. . . . For writing involves containment. Like all art, it takes place within limits. . . . If it is thought of as happening within a frame, the frame may be hacked at by a true genius (and only by a true genius) but it must not be broken by any man. The writing cannot be made to take the place of the world. The world will remain in its own sprawl.
> (John Ciardi, "On Writing and Bad Writing," *Saturday Review*, December 15, 1962)

During her college years and immediately after, Margaret Wemyss' involvement with "The Winnipeg Old Left" was of prime importance in establishing her convictions about the relation of men and women to social structures. The dynamic for change and reform that had been a founding factor of the CCF party in the thirties was still strong. The group, composed of members of the CCF, the CCP, and their followers, believed passionately in the brotherhood of man and the urgency for social reform. The "Grace before Meat" that J. S. Woodsworth had written for the use of Labour families carried their convictions and their commitment:

> We are thankful for these and all the good things of life. We recognize that they are part of the common heritage and come to us through the efforts of our brothers and sisters the world over. What we desire for ourselves we wish for all. To this end may we take our share in the world's work and the world's struggles.

To one of her own generation, the most readily identifiable western Canadian quality about Margaret Laurence is her early dedication to social reform and the continued, basic, social awareness that is part of the foundation of all her work. Growing up with a troubled knowledge that the Depression had cramped—or defeated—their parents' generation, and coming to maturity with the knowledge that everywhere in the Western world their generation's choices were predetermined by the Second World War, she and her associates saw concerted social action as the hope and the only protection for mankind. Margaret Laurence's profound awareness of men and women constrained by social structures, exploiting others through these structures, and themselves being exploited, was set at this time. Her statements of concern were to become a part of the fabric of all her fiction.

She graduated from United College in 1947 at the age of twenty-one and for about a year worked as a reporter on *The Winnipeg Citizen*, an experience that gave her a lasting wariness of newspaper work as favourable training-ground for the apprentice fiction writer. Writing book reviews and a daily radio column, besides covering all labour news, she was far too busy and weary at night to practise her own writing. But she did develop competence in the tools of her trade—in typing and in writing skilfully to deadlines. And her work with labour and union men both consolidated her social and political convictions and personalized them; from theoretical ideology she advanced to the problems of individuals, individually perceived.

Her experience of Africa, between 1950 and 1957, acted as a kind of dynamic culture-shock, a catalyst, on the talents of Margaret Laurence. In 1948 she and Jack Laurence, a civil engineering graduate of the University of Manitoba, were married. They left Canada in 1949 for England, and they left England for Africa in 1950. Jack Laurence was in charge of a dam-building project in the British Protectorate of Somaliland, now Somalia. In 1952 they moved to the Gold Coast, now Ghana, where they lived until 1957. The Laurence's daughter, Jocelyn, was born during a leave in England in 1952; their son, David, was born in Ghana in 1955. *A Tree for Poverty* (1954), *The Tomorrow-Tamer* (1963), *This Side Jordan* (1960), and *The Prophet's Camel Bell* (1963) are all works immediate to the experience of Africa, and *Long Drums and Cannons* (1968) is the outcome of a decade of understanding and admiration for the literature of emergent West Africa. Of these works, however, only *A Tree for Poverty*, a collection of translations of Somali tales and poems, some of *The Tomorrow-Tamer* stories, notably "Drummer of All the World," published by *Queen's Quarterly* in 1956, and a part of *This Side Jordan*, were actually written in Africa. The rest came from experience assimilated, distanced, and distilled into fictional form after the Laurences returned to Vancouver in 1957 and, in the case of *The Prophet's Camel Bell*, from journal material reworked and reordered.

The Prophet's Camel Bell predates in its content any of Margaret Laurence's other published works; though written in 1962 and published in 1963, it recounts the experiences of the Laurences in Somaliland between 1950 and 1952. As a travel-memoir it is relatively self-determined in its form; one is tempted to call its genre the least demanding of those in which Margaret Laurence has worked. She, however, calls it "the most difficult thing I ever wrote." Fiction has always been the centre of her artistic interest: "I believe that fiction is more true than fact," she says, and when working in any other area, she feels she is using her left hand only. However, because of its biographical information and because of its core theme—the description of her own growth in self-awareness and humility in the experience of an alien culture—*The Prophet's Camel Bell* provides a logical starting point for a consideration of all her work.

When she wrote the book ten years after the experiences it deals with, she found that her diaries were not usable in the form in which they had been written: "I refer to them a lot, but essentially [I] had to try to go back in my mind and re-create the situation, while also trying to understand it at a distance of ten years." In the text of the book itself she demonstrates her frustration with the diary's relative uselessness; she also charts stages in the growth of her self-knowledge:

> In my diary, I recorded that it was surprising to find the ease with which "one gains their popularity" by showing friendliness and courtesy towards them. The Somalis, I went on to say, speaking generally but referring to Abdi, were good judges of character (naturally, they must be, since they appeared to like me) and one of the chief ways in which they judged Europeans was whether or not the Europeans liked them. A later, much later, comment at the end of this paragraph bears in heavy lead-pencil one word—*Bosh*. It was not all bosh, however—what I had really indicated by the initial statement was that I myself tended to judge people on whether or not I felt they liked me.
>
> (*The Prophet's Camel Bell,* p. 182)

Before going to Somaliland, the Laurences had read all the literature they could find, from Colonial Office pamphlets which were several decades out of date, through history they "ferreted from libraries," but which had only "a limited meaning for us, despite its power to stir the imagination with past glory or disgrace, the tramplings of time over one corner of the earth" (*The Prophet's Camel Bell,* p. 4). They had read of the travels of Sir Richard Burton, of the other early explorers and conquerors, and of the many men and women who had been driven across the land and sold to the slave-traders:

> Somaliland was the end of a bitter journey at the beginning of a lifetime of bondage, for there the Arab slave routes had emerged at the sea, and from there the dhow-loads of slaves had once been shipped across the Gulf of Aden to be sold in the flesh markets of Arabia. . . .
>   We read of these events and pondered them. But they could not tell us what we would find there now.   (*The Prophet's Camel Bell*, p. 5)

Later, sorting and ordering her African memories, Margaret Laurence did more reading, to confirm, explain, and enlarge her impressions and perceptions. O. Mannoni's *Prospero and Caliban: A Study of The Psychology of Colonization* had a special and lasting impact on her, providing, she says, the "shock of recognition one sometimes feels when another's words have a specific meaning in terms of one's own experience." The influence of Mannoni has reached far beyond *The Prophet's Camel Bell* in her work; its theme is her theme of exile; its studies of colonizer and colonial, of ruler and dependant, both suggest and confirm the emotional situations and their psychological bases that she has worked out in the lives of many of her characters. Mannoni's study informs "Voices of Adamo," for instance, in Adamo's tragic, mistaken, psychological dependency on Captain Fossey, the regimental band master; Mannoni's work also gives a depth of tragic inevitability to the generations back of Jules Tonnerre in *The Diviners*.

Only the Bible has had so obviously a continuing influence on Margaret Laurence's work:

> But I had gone ill-provided with reading material and had paced the hotel room until I discovered in a dressing-table drawer the ubiquitous Gideons Bible

and read for the first time in my life the five books of
Moses. Of all the books which I might have chosen to
read just then, few would have been more to the
point, for the Children of Israel were people of the
desert, as the Somalis were, and fragments from
those books were to return to me again and again.
*And there was no water for the people to drink—and
the people thirsted.* Or, when we were to wonder
how the tribesmen could possibly live and maintain
hope through the season of drought—*in the
wilderness, where thou hast seen how that the Lord
Thy God bare thee, as a man doth bear his son, in all
the way that ye went.* Or the verse that remained
with me most of all, when at last and for the first time
I was myself a stranger in a strange land, and was
sometimes given hostile words and was also given,
once, food and shelter in a time of actual need, by
tribesmen who had little enough for themselves—*Thou shalt not oppress a stranger, for ye
know the heart of a stranger, seeing ye were
strangers in the land of Egypt.*

> (*The Prophet's Camel Bell*, p. 9)

That final text could serve well as an epigraph to all the works of
Margaret Laurence: she perceives individuals as strangers in a
strange land and her effort has been, throughout, to know and
to show "the heart of a stranger." Magnificent in the stories it
tells and even more haunting in those left unfinished, the
Bible's influence pervades all her fiction. Sometimes she
builds her own symbolic meanings from its stories—Hagar and
Ishmael, or Rachel mourning for her children. Often she uses
its language in phrases or whole verses. Especially, and over all
her writing, there is the sense of awe and mystery so strong as
one reads the Old Testament—of large events moving strangely beyond man's comprehending, and of man moving, somehow, onward through them despite his small understanding of
their purpose or meaning. There is also in all of her writing,

though particularly marked in *The Diviners,* a New Testament sense of the mysterious, but inexhaustible presence of God's grace.

Margaret and Jack Laurence spent the years between 1950 and 1952 in the British protectorate of Somaliland, where Jack Laurence was building some thirty reservoirs, or *ballehs,* over an area of 6,500 square miles: "The Engineer will be required to carry out all reconnaissance and detailed survey, to do all calculations and designs, to be responsible for expenditure and the supervision of staff and plant." It was a challenging and daunting assignment, but one that attracted Jack Laurence because, "he felt a need to work for once on a job that plainly needed doing—not a paved road to replace a gravel one, but a road where none had been before." And Margaret was permitted to go along in spite of the polite demurrings of the Colonial Office who had no accommodation available for married couples. She was permitted to go, in fact, because her husband gave a striking description of her as "an accomplished woodswoman, a kind of female Daniel Boone." For the first, but by no means the last time, she took advantage of an attitude first voiced by Mohamed, their Somali servant, but widespread among the Somalis and greatly to the Laurences' advantage: " 'Canadian peoples different,' he would say, and this covered a multitude of lapses."

On its plain narrative level *The Prophet's Camel Bell* is the story of what the Laurences found in Somaliland and what they did there. In the face of the predictable and understandable distrust of the Somali tribesmen, still caught in their age-old, nomadic patterns of society, the dams were finally built in a desert country that has no temperate weather, but only drought, downpour, and a brief, beautiful flowering of the land. The Laurences did not stay to see all of them completed; when his two-year term was over, Jack Laurence relinquished the final stages of the project to a Somali engineer. But before they left Somaliland they were able to go out into the desert to see *Balleh Gihli,* the *Balleh* of the Camels, filled with water:

Around the edges of the *balleh,* the camels milled and drank, led by tribesmen whose faces expressed nothing except the desire to get their beasts watered and back to the encampment. Somali women and girls hitched up their robes around their knees and waded into the *balleh* to fill their water vessels, which they then placed upon their heads and sauntered off with barely a glance in our direction.

Hersi [the Laurences' servant], snorting with angry laughter, came back from a consultation with a group of tribesmen. He threw up his hands in mock despair.

"I am not knowing what kind of people these bush people. They saying—what is these *Ingrese* doing here, beside our *balleh*?"

It was their *balleh* now. They had assimilated it; it belonged here.   (*The Prophet's Camel Bell*, p. 235)

Deeper and far more important to Margaret Laurence than the story of events is the story of her voyage into an awareness of the Somali people: "It was not a matter of intelligence, but of viewing the whole of life through different eyes." Their land was harsh and their lives demanded from them qualities of acceptance and endurance that she had never imagined, much less confronted:

In that assembly of wealth and want, of kings and *fellaheen*, praying for strength in the month of fasting, the tribesmen in the Somali desert also knelt, unaware that they were among the least blessed of Allah's subjects. Their worship was as bare and lacking in outward splendour as their lives. Their mosques were circles of brushwood, their ritual ablution waters the brackish dregs of mud pools or simply the sand, their religious relics the memory of graves abandoned in the desert. . . . Faith to them was as necessary as life, inevitable as death. They looked up and knew the Word had been made visible.   (*The Prophet's Camel Bell*, p. 86)

On its most significant level, *The Prophet's Camel Bell* is the record of an enormous and forever unfinished exercise in understanding: "Our voyage began some years ago. When can a voyage be said to have ended? When you reach the place you were bound for, presumably. But sometimes your destination turns out to be quite other than you expected." It is the pervading sense of the author's developing understanding that differentiates this book from scores of well-written, entertaining travel-memoirs whose themes and movements are anecdotal and geographical only.

The fiction writer's urge to characterize, to dramatize, to show the modifications that experience effects on personality, is as central to this work as to Margaret Laurence's novels. A character quickly emerges in her narrative, a *persona* of herself, whose energy, variety, and growth dominate the book. The complete span of her maturing is suggested as the book begins:

> Nothing can equal in hope and apprehension the first voyage east of Suez, yourself eager for all manner of oddities, pretending to disbelieve in marvels lest you appear naïve but anticipating them just the same, prepared for anything, prepared for nothing, burdened with baggage—most of it useless, unburdened by knowledge, assuming all will go well because it is you and not someone else going to the far place (harm comes only to others), bland as eggplant and as innocent of the hard earth as a fledgling sparrow. . . .
>
> And in the excitement at the trip, the last thing in the world that would occur to you is that the strangest glimpses you may have of any creature in the distant lands will be those you catch of yourself.
>
> (*The Prophet's Camel Bell*, p. 1)

The fast-paced sentence of that first quoted paragraph, piling phrase on phrase to climax in a pair of similes that are entirely apt, totally familiar, and as positive and satisfying in their rhythm as a final clash of major chords, is a hallmark of Margaret Laurence's early style. So is the passage's final aphoristic generalization, both in its epigrammatic "moral" and in its rhythm. It is unmistakably North American, in the tradition whose origins lie in the habits of mind and the speech patterns of a pioneer people and whose literary antecedents lie in the works of Franklin, Haliburton, and Mark Twain.

These particular qualities of her style are successful agents in immediately projecting to the reader a character of energy and decision, wit and sensitivity—although the self-characterization is at first awkward and self-conscious compared to the sureness with which she establishes her later fiction's central figures. As she begins to build her sense of spiritual growth into her prose, however, our impressions are both amplified and modified. The familiar, almost caricature-figure of the naïve traveller shifts towards a character whose dominant qualities are understanding and control:

> I had flair, but no patience. Everything had to be done right away, this minute. . . .
>   I stopped my buzzing after a while and looked around, and then I noticed that everything was calm. The land was not aware of me. I might enter its quietness or not, just as I chose. Hesitantly at first, because it had been my pride to be as perpetually busy as an escalator, I entered. Then I realized how much I had needed Sheikh, how I had been moving towards it.   (*The Prophet's Camel Bell*, p. 27)

She describes her growth in humility through a forcing-ground of self-doubt. Her early, enthusiastic doctoring of the Somali with aspirin and "number nines" gives way to appalled self-questioning as a Somali herdsman, nearly dead from thirst, crawls into their camp:

> What had I known of life here at all? . . . it seemed to me that I had been a child, playing doctor with candy

pills, not knowing—not really knowing—that the
people that I was treating were not dolls. Had I
wanted to help them for their sake or for my own?
Had I needed their gratitude so much?

For a while after that day, I could not stand to
look at my toy potions and powders. I shoved the tin
box under a camp cot. I would have no more to do
with it. Then I saw that this way, too, was an
exaggeration. Would I do nothing simply because I
could not do everything? The searching sun of the
Jilal exposed not only the land but the heart as well.

(*The Prophet's Camel Bell*, p. 63)

In the book's first paragraph she sketches her dream of the
exotic East, replete with "elephants old as forests," "apes like
jesters," and "men who can change into leopards at the flick of
a claw." But the realities of Africa were often harsher and more
violent than her most fantastic imaginings, and she paints the
strange landscape vividly in its various moods and seasons. Her
set-descriptions are richly sense-gratifying, with a strongly
marked rhythm, an interweaving of sound patterns, and a
strong sense of colour and composition. They stop the flow of
the narrative to place us in a particular setting, as here, in a
description of the rain-renewed land:

The cactus plants had put forth yellow waxen
blossoms, and on the hills all kinds of wild flowers
grew. The wilted aloes had filled with moisture and
become succulently firm again, rosettes of broad
pointed leaves mottled green and brown, edged with
rust-coloured barbs like a shark's teeth, and in the
centre a thin stalk culminating in a scarlet flower,
really a cluster of innumerable tiny flowers. Weird
insects emerged—a crimson beetle patterned in gold
and black, looking like a small heraldic shield, and
another that looked like a piece of Italian mosaic, a
delicate turquoise with pastel markings in coral. Near
the stony river-bed the green pigeons had returned

to the gnarled fig tree.

(*The Prophet's Camel Bell*, p. 48)

Equally precise in its observation of the object but remarkably different in its bare effectiveness is the language describing a Somali tribesman against the desert landscape:

> The land was incredibly empty, the sky open from one side of the horizon to the other. The light brown sand glistened with mica and slid down into long ribbed dunes. It seemed to be no place for any living thing. Even the thorny bushes, digging their roots in and finding nourishment in that inhospitable soil, appeared to have a precarious hold on life, as though at any moment they might relax their grip, dry up entirely and be blown clear away.
>
> But the land was not empty. A figure appeared, standing against the sky, a Somali herdsman, very straight and calm, looking at us with a haughty detachment. He wore a brownish orange robe, cotton that might once have been white but had taken on the colour of the muddy water from the wells where the camels drank. He carried his spear across one shoulder. Around him his sheep clustered, spindly legged creatures, white with ebony heads and no wool at all, only short hair like a deer's hide. He did not move or turn his head as we jolted dustily past him. To him, we might have been as ephemeral as dust-devils, the columns of wind and sand that swirled across the desert and then disappeared without a trace.   (*The Prophet's Camel Bell*, p. 20)

Several self-contained chapters of characterization-narrative, each one like a short story in itself, form a group towards the end of the book, loosely framed by the story of the Laurences' early experiences in Somaliland and rounded off by the completion of the *balleh* and their farewell to the desert country. The book loses the unity of its narrative progression through their insertion, but it would be a comparatively meagre work without them: the humanity, vitality, and wit, not only of the Somali characterizations, but also of the vignette-drawings of the English as Margaret Laurence gradually understands them and so modifies her prejudice against them, add far more to the substance of the work than they take away from its form.

Among these chapters is the story of "Hersi Half-tongue," orator, actor, and poet, whose dream it was to be part of the powerful realm of clubs and bookkeepers, but who was only educated enough to act as the Laurences' interpreter. The story of Abdi, the faithful servant who turned enemy, shows his betrayal and bitterness both as a measure of the ever-threatening abyss between one culture and another, and as an ironic commentary on man's unawareness of the depths of the differences between himself and any other man. Several of these stories end on a carefully prepared, effectively staged note of pathos and irony, the elements held in a nice balance. Hersi's tale ends this way:

> Out in the Haud, when the tales are told around the fire, perhaps the thin unimpressive figure still rises and begins, with his flawed speech, to build in words the caliph's palace and the enchanter's tower. . . .
> And he becomes the people in the tale, the great Wiil Waal who drove the last of the Galla kings from Jigjigga, or Ahmed the miserable woodseller who—wondrously—married a sultan's daughter.
> (*The Prophet's Camel Bell*, p. 160)

And in Abdi's chapter, there is a frankly sentimental finish, fitting for the story of the old man whose relationship to the Laurences ended with failure on both sides and, certainly on theirs, with regret:

> In Paradise, the Qoran says, there are gardens where the fountains flow eternally and where the faithful may recline on divans and be attended by love-

ly women for ever and ever. A desert dweller's heaven, the heaven of Islam. But for some of the sons of the desert, I do not think this heaven will be quite enough. If I believed I would wish there to be battles somewhere in Paradise, for an old warrior who never knew—and who probably could not have borne to know—that his truest and most terrible battle, like all men's, was with himself.

(*The Prophet's Camel Bell*, p. 189)

Margaret Laurence found her own work to do in Somaliland: she had quickly become intrigued by the extensive oral literature of the Somali people and she began the task of finding and translating examples of the folk-tales, the love-poems or *belwo*, and the more formal, highly disciplined and developed poems called *gabei*:

Although they have no written language, the Somalis are a nation of poets. In the evenings, around the camp fires, the men sing and tell stories far into the night. And in the *magala*, or town, they gather in the tea shops and often several *gabei* poets will spend hours chanting their own poetry, listened to by a large audience. This country is lacking in almost all materials needed for painting and sculpture, and in any event the Somalis, being Muslims, are not in favour of making "images." But stories and poems require no special materials other than the talent of the person concerned. . . . Although the life of the Somali camel-herder is drab and harsh, in their poetry and stories one finds sensitivity, intelligence, earthy humour, and a delight in lovely clothes and lovely women. . . .

Literary Somali is a superstructure erected on the foundation of everyday speech. A vast number of words are never used except in poetry, and these

have a subtle and precise meaning. Often an amazing
amount of information is compressed into one word.
(The Prophet's Camel Bell, p. 190)

Margaret Laurence's translations, *A Tree For Poverty*
(the title taken from a famous *gabei*), were done in 1952 and
published in 1954 under the auspices of the British
Protectorate of Somaliland. Ironically, as with many others
whom she met, the administrator who hounded officialdom for
a grant to publish her translations was not the cold "imperialist" she had first imagined him to be:

Discussing it, all at once he pointed to one page and
spoke with an unexpected intensity.
"It would be worthwhile for this one passage in
your introduction," he said, "even if there were
nothing else in the book."
The passage was a description of the Somali
tribesmen's harrowing and precarious life in the dry
Jilal. I realized then how deep was his attachment to
this land and these people.
(The Prophet's Camel Bell, p. 225)

The work of translating had to begin with the effort of
erasing the strong Somali prejudice against telling the stories
and poems to any foreigner, let alone a woman; then of listening, transcribing, and reworking to catch as far as possible the
tones and shades of meaning of the tellers. She had several
helpers, among them Musa Galaal and B. W. Andrzejewski,
who were scholars and researchers into Somali literature. But
most important to her work were the stories Hersi Half-tongue
told her, for he not only told her the tales he knew, he also
gathered material for her from many other storytellers and he
acted them all out in front of her.
When Margaret Laurence worked at these translations in
1952, she already had the patience and the discipline of a

professional writer—qualities to be seen everywhere in the translations, but particularly in the plain, expository style of her introduction to the book. This introduction is an exercise in restraint, for her own writing is characterized by its colour and intensity. Her purpose as she states it is simply to record poems which, because of the brevity of the life of a poem in oral literature and among a nomadic people, will otherwise be lost in another fifty years. The tales and stories "must be accepted for what they are—not the accumulation of the writings of centuries, but the stories of a highly imaginative race without a written language." The poem *"Qaraami"* (Passion), for instance, is a *gabei* composed about 1937 by a young poet called Elmi Bonderii, who is said to have died for love of a young woman whom he could not marry because of his poverty. The poem tells of his love for the beautiful Baar for whom, in the poem only, the poet has divorced his wife. It is a work of some seventy lines; three stanzas demonstrate its simplicity and strength, in the quality of the devotion it projects and in the pride of the lover for his conquest:

She is like the girl that Qaabiil and Haabiil loved,
And over whom they fought, and both were slain;
Or like that Qanso of the Ogaden,
Whose suitors came from two opposing tribes,
And in their battles a thousand warriors died.
But nowadays, no man could hope to find
A woman of equal charm, except Quduro
Whose fairness is famed throughout the entire land.

Consider how Baar appears in her richest garb,
With finely polished slippers of soft wood,
Rare leather amulets, and silken scarf.
Necklace of amber, blue and scarlet robes,
And silver rings that glow with amethysts.
When she is clad like this, and sits near me,
I look at her from the corner of my eyes,
And want to see no other thing on earth,
So deep my happiness at seeing her.

But comeliness is not her only gift—
Her strong hands weave the mats and tend the fire;
Swiftly she works, with every task well done.
She is the one who gives her parents pride,
She is dear to them—ah, yes and expensive, too!
For her sake one whole family I destroyed—
That is to say, when I divorced my wife
And broke our dwelling-place to marry Baar.

(*A Tree For Poverty*, p. 41)

Margaret Laurence's introductory passages on the element of the grotesque in the Somali tales, and on the strong sense of drama which carries over from the people to their literature, are particularly interesting in view of her own future work. Arawailo, the great queen with an insane hatred of men, and Deg-Der, the cannibal woman, are Grotesques in Somali literature as Hagar Shipley is a Canadian Grotesque. Deg-Der's story is particularly effective in its combination of spare, suspenseful story-telling and blood-chilling content:

One day the husband came home and found the door of their dwelling barred against him.

"What is this?" he cried, astounded. "Does my own wife bar the door against me?"

But his wife would not open the door.

"Now then," he said, "if I go and kill a fat sheep for our meal tonight, will you open the door?"

But his wife would still not open the door.

"Suppose I kill a fat camel," the husband pleaded, "the best of my herd, and you may cook the meat for your meal. Will you open the door then?"

But still his wife refused.

Then the husband's face grew wan with fear.

"And if I kill you a fat . . . boy?" he asked.

But the wife would still not unbar the door.

Then the husband's brow grew tight with anxiety.

"And if I kill you a fat . . . girl?" he asked.

But the door remained closed.

Then the husband's heart grew pale with dread.

"If you want none of these things for your meal," he said, "perhaps the one you hunger for is . . . myself?"

And then the third daughter of Deg-Der opened the door and met him.

(*A Tree For Poverty*, p. 133)

The experience of translating these Somali poems and tales gave exercise to the strong, but at that time almost dormant quality of the storyteller in Margaret Laurence's own temperament. At the same time the experience of living for two years in Somaliland confirmed and established her perceptions and convictions about the dignity of men and women, their qualities of survival, and their need for freedom of the spirit which have been central to all her work since. Africa gave her distance from her Canadian experience, the opportunity to move out from it, to distance it in an utterly alien context, and to let it develop its own life within her so that later it was possible for it all to grow into her books.

It seemed to me that my feeling of regret arose from unwisely loving a land where I must always remain a stranger. But it was also possible that my real reason for loving it was simply because I was an outsider here. One can never be a stranger in one's own land—it is precisely this fact which makes it so difficult to live there.

(*The Prophet's Camel Bell*, p. 227)

On the deepest level of all she perceived in herself and in all her relations with the Somalis what Sir Thomas Browne had perceived long ago, "There is all Africa and her prodigies in us." The years of the early fifties were the exploring, finding, and confirming years for Margaret Laurence. The final writing of *The Prophet's Camel Bell* was done long after, in Vancouver in 1962, at a watershed point in her life, just before she moved to England. At that time *This Side Jordan* and *The Tomorrow-Tamer* had been published, and the first draft of *The Stone Angel* had been written. Margaret Laurence was then fully committed to a career as a writer. The writing of *The Prophet's Camel Bell* marked the end of the apprenticeship experiences that the years in Africa had given her; the book was her acknowledgement of that apprenticeship and her farewell to it.

THREE

"Departures II"
The Tomorrow-Tamer;
This Side Jordan

In 1952 the Laurences went to the Gold Coast where they stayed until 1957, the year it became the independent nation of Ghana. The nine stories that make up *The Tomorrow-Tamer* were written and published singly between 1954 and 1962 and then collected and published by McClelland and Stewart of Canada and by Macmillan of England in 1963. "Drummer Of All The World," the first story, was written in 1954 and published in 1956 in *Queen's Quarterly* through the good judgement of Malcolm Ross, its editor. The other stories appeared in journals as different in status and circulation as the University of British Columbia's *Prism, The Saturday Evening Post*, and Macmillan's own annual collection of stories, *Winter's Tales. This Side Jordan*, which won the Beta Sigma Phi prize for a first novel by a Canadian, was written in Ghana and Vancouver between 1955 and 1960 and published in 1960 by McClelland and Stewart in Canada and by Macmillan in England.

Both the stories and the novel are set in Ghana just before independence; they demonstrate from many angles the effects of the processes of independence on individual Ghanaians and on the bewildered, anxious Europeans who were caught up in the hopes and the despairs of emergent nationhood. More than that, they give constant evidence of the enormous impact of

Africa and her African experiences on the creative talents of Margaret Laurence. Seldom has "culture shock" had such a positive outcome; in the ranks of Canadian writers one would need to go back to Susanna Moodie to find a counterpart, an Englishwoman whose experience of Upper Canada in the 1830's jolted her into the creative energy that her *Roughing It In The Bush* (1852) displays. There, however, the analogy ends, for Susanna Moodie's powers were strong, but fragmented and finally unrealized; in contrast there is a quality of form and finish in *The Tomorrow-Tamer* stories and a consistent pace and energy in *This Side Jordan* which point with assurance to the continuous development that Margaret Laurence's subsequent work has displayed.

Technically the stories are strong: only "The Pure Diamond Man," written in 1962 after Margaret Laurence's interests had moved strongly towards the novel, is less successful than all the others in its matching of voice to character and form to substance. The question of form in fiction, she says, has always occupied her a good deal before she starts to write:

> One wants to figure out some form which will express the characters in the best way one can . . . the characters and their situations tend to develop in one's mind simultaneously with the verbal forms which will convey them. . . .
>
> The problem of form, it seems to me, is always the problem of selection—how to discover the structure which will provide the best skeleton for this particular flesh and will help to make the process of selection more possible. I don't think of the form as something imposed upon a novel, but as its bone, the skeleton which makes it possible for the flesh to move and be revealed as itself.

In *The Tomorrow-Tamer* stories Margaret Laurence has resolved her search for form, for "the best skeleton for this particular flesh," in two ways. One of them is the swift-paced, dramatically structured short story; it consists of several "scenes," with an action rising to a climax and rounded off, subdued in a final ironic clinching sentence or a brief reflective epilogue which casts its implications back in review over the whole story. The other might be called a "tale"; it owes more to traditional narrative methods of the oral storyteller than to the artfulness of a verbal edifice designed for the printed page. Though the tale has, indeed, its high dramatic moments its essential effect does not depend on them, nor on any element of surprise or suspense. Rather, an inevitability of outcome, a measured inexorability of events like some process of nature, is the cumulative and ultimately satisfying force in the tales even though its manifestations may well be tragic.

Of the first group, and these stories are the more numerous, "The Drummer of All the World" exemplifies the form at its most effective. It is constructed in nine "scenes" and an epilogue. The story is told by Matthew, the son of an English missionary, who has grown up in Africa, has come back after a ten-year absence and Ghana's independence, and will shortly be leaving again, this time forever. For seven scenes he remembers his boyhood and youth; each is a small entity, signalled in type by a double-spacing between the ending of one and the beginning of the next scene. Each scene marks off a development in Matthew's awareness; some of these were significant to the boy as the events happened, some are only now significant to the remembering man. Matthew's memories of his father, a stern, godly man in the Old Testament image, who "thought he was bringing Salvation to Africa," and of his pale, tired mother are thin beside the memories of his warmly vital relationship with Yaa, his African nurse and foster-mother. Matthew grew up with Yaa's son, Kwabena, almost—but not quite—as a brother. Yaa's niece, Afua, was his first experience of girlhood and his first love. Each scene makes its point, sometimes with a circular movement from its initial statement to its final one: "My father was an idol-breaker of the old school. . . . But I was ashamed. I still am. Moses broke the idols of his own people" (*The Tomorrow-Tamer*, p. 4). And in another scene, "the parades were something my parents organized and bore with, but never liked. . . . 'Religion is not fun,' thundered my father. 'It is serving God' " (*The Tomorrow-Tamer*, p. 5).

Matthew balanced precariously between the missionary world of his home and the real world of Africa that he knew through Yaa and Kwabena. He owed duty to one, he felt, and therefore he experienced guilt for his betrayal of it; but his love was given to the other, the African world, and his most precious experiences were of that:

> When I was with Kwabena, the world of the mission and Band of Jesus did not exist for me. However powerfully my father preached, he could not stop the drums playing in the evenings. Kwabena and I would sit under the casuarina tree in our garden and listen to the thudding rhythm, the tempo building up and up until you knew the drummer was hypnotised with the sound.
>
> "Ei! That one! It is almost like the voice of Drum himself," Kwabena would say. And I would imagine the vast-bellied giant, the Drummer of all the world, drumming on himself, the Drum of drums. For years I thought of the great grinning mask each time the drums pulsed in the moon-grey night, seeming to shiver even the ribboned leaves of the banana palms.
>
> The casuarina tree was a special meeting-place for Kwabena and me. It was there the wind spoke to us, whispering through the feather fans of the branches like the warning voices of the ancestors themselves. It was there that Kwabena used to tell me stories about Ananse Kokuroko, Ananse the gigantic spider, who desired greedily all power and all wealth, and who wove his web of cunning to ensnare the stupid and the guileless.
>
> (*The Tomorrow-Tamer*, p. 7)

Finally, his childhood's experience of Africa culminates in his youthful possession of Afua: "possessing her, I possessed all earth."

Then scenes eight and nine describe Matthew's return to the new Ghana after ten years away:

> The country was to have its independence the follow-
> ing year, but the quality of change was more than
> political. It was so many things. It was an old chieftain
> in a greasy and threadbare robe with no retinue—
> only a small boy carrying aloft the red umbrella,
> ancient mark of aristocracy. It was an African night-
> club called "Weekend in Wyoming," and a
> mahogany-skinned girl wearing white face powder.
> It was parades of a new sort, buxom market-women
> chanting "Free-dom!" (*The Tomorrow-Tamer*, p. 13)

Both Afua and Kwabena and, through them, Ghana itself and all its people reject Matthew; Afua with "I greet you—mas-ter," and hatred in her eyes, and Kwabena with a defensive resentment that shocks and cuts both of them:

> "Why should they tell you"—he smiled wryly—"if an
> old African woman dies?"
>   Pain and anger spread like a bloodstain over my
> whole mind.
>   "You know as well as I do," I replied harshly,
> "that she was more mother to me than my own
> mother."
>   Kwabena looked at me as if he hated me.
>   "Yes," he said, "I shared my mother with you, in
> exchange for your cast-off khaki shorts."
>   (*The Tomorrow-Tamer,* p. 16)

In the epilogue Matthew gropes through his pain and disillusion towards some new area of self-knowledge. Here, as in some of the individual scenes, there is a unifying connection between the first of "The Drummer of All the World" and its ending. It begins with: "My father thought he was bringing Salvation to Africa. I, on the other hand, no longer know what salvation is. I am not sure that it lies in the future. And I know

now that it is not to be found in the past." The echoing lines come near the end of the story, but they have a significant progression: "My father thought he was bringing Salvation to Africa. I do not any longer know what salvation is. I only know that one man cannot find it for another man, and one land cannot bring it to another."

"The Tomorrow-Tamer" and "The Voices of Adamo" have an open-ended quality that differentiates their effect from that of the tight and circular pattern of "The Drummer of All the World." To call them "tales" in differentiation from "short stories" is simply to recognize their root in oral, rather than written story-telling techniques. Margaret Laurence herself indicates this in the final lines of "The Tomorrow-Tamer":

> Many tales were woven around his name, but they ended always in the same way, always the same.
> "The fish is netted and eaten; the antelope is hunted and fed upon; the python is slain and cast into the cooking-pot. But—oh, my children, my sons—a man consumed by the gods lives forever."
> *(The Tomorrow-Tamer*, p. 104)

Kofi in "The Tomorrow-Tamer" dedicated himself to the bridge he helped to build, as a priest dedicates himself to his God. He could not understand or contemplate his life without service to the bridge, and the need for his service was thus threatened by Emmanuel's uncomprehending question: "Do you think it needs looking after?" Strong in his own conviction that men in far places would always celebrate him as a bridgeman, he volunteered to paint the highest steel girders to celebrate his power. Then, forgetting a bridgeman's caution, he walked fearlessly and needlessly out on the catwalk, looked straight into the sun, slipped, and "arched into the river like a thrown spear."

> "What could have possessed the idiot?" the Superintendent cried, in anger and anguish, for it was the only fatal accident on the job.

"He did not believe that the bridge would hurt him, perhaps," Badu said.

"Did he think it was alive?" Wain said despairingly. "Won't they ever learn?" . . .

As for the people of Owurasu, they were not surprised. They understood perfectly well what had happened. The bridge, clearly, had sacrificed its priest in order to appease the river. The people felt they knew the bridge now.

(*The Tomorrow-Tamer*, p. 103)

The tragic crux of "The Voices of Adamo" is loss. Adamo has lost his family, the warmth and refreshment of his mother, the sureness of his father, the security of his tribal home, and the other side of security's coin, the hard but necessary learning of fear and caution: "But the fears were not the greater part. As long as the laws were kept, the palms and the dark river and the red earth were to Adamo like his own brothers, who would not forsake him." Without his family, his village, and his tribe, Adamo has no identity; he is like a lost spirit of the dead, until he finds a place as drummer in a Regimental Band. He gives his total devotion and loyalty to the band and in return, naturally, he expects the security of his lost home, his former place in family, village, and tribe. When he is discharged from the band and the regiment, he thinks that he has been betrayed by Captain Fossey, the band master, through whom he has unknowingly applied for discharge papers. Because he is totally uncomprehending and because the security he thought he had found is his basic need and the only means of his personal and spiritual survival, he kills the captain.

When Major Appiah, an African officer, comes to prepare him for the court-marshal and its inevitable verdict, Adamo's confused anguish culminates in the question "I will stay?"

"Yes," Major Appiah said, and as he spoke he became aware of a crippling sense of weariness, as though an accumulation of centuries had been foisted upon

himself, to deal with somehow. "You can stay,
Adamo. You can stay as long as you live."
(The Tomorrow-Tamer, p. 224)

"The Voices of Adamo" illustrates more clearly than any other
story in the collection the bonds of interdependency that are
unwittingly forged by colonists and colonials, the relationships
that are damaging, crucial, and often, as in this case,
destructive to both sides. Captain Fossey had no way either of
understanding Adamo's expectations of him or of fulfilling
those expectations. This is the story in which Margaret
Laurence most clearly demonstrates the thesis of Mannoni's
work, *Prospero and Caliban: The Psychology of Colonization.*

All *The Tomorrow-Tamer* stories are built from the point
of view of the ironist—not the ironist who assumes superiority
of understanding or sophistication of intellect and so con-
descends to her subjects and characters, but the ironist who
sees at once the immense vitality and the enormous con-
tradictions of joy and pain, hopes and achievements, among
the people of an emergent nation. Margaret Laurence has
sketched her own attitude of mind during the time she was
writing her African stories:

> They were written out of the milieu of a rapidly-
> changing colonialism and the emerging in-
> dependence of African countries. They are not
> entirely hopeful books, nor do they, I think, ignore
> some of the inevitable casualties of social change,
> both African and European, but they do reflect the
> predominantly optimistic outlook of many Africans
> and many Western liberals in the later 1950's and
> early 1960's. ("Ten Year's Sentences,"
> Canadian Literature, 41 (Summer 1969): 10)

The first and most essential challenge to any writer is to
find the right "voice" for his material. In every one of these
stories, the main character is in some large sense an outsider.
Some of the stories have a first-person narrator and some a

third, but in every case Margaret Laurence herself, irrevocably an outsider to Africa, can readily identify with the particular person who tells the story or about whom the story is told. So it is when Matthew speaks his farewell to Africa, out of the sadness and rejection of his present:

> I shall be leaving soon. Leaving the surf that stretches up long white fingers to clutch the brown land. The fetid village enclosed and darkened by a green sky of overhanging palm trees. The giant heartbeat of the night drums. The flame tree whose beauty is suddenly splendid—and short-lived—like the beauty of African women. The little girl dancing with her shadow in the stifling streets. The child sleeping, unmindful, while flies caress his eyes and mouth with the small bright wings of decay. The squalor, the exaltation, the pain. I shall be leaving it all.
>
> But—oh Kwabena, do you think I will ever forget?   (*The Tomorrow-Tamer*, p. 19)

In "The Merchant of Heaven," Will Ketteridge, who has been long enough in Africa to know and to accept that he will be always essentially an alien, tells the story of Brother Lemon who comes to Africa as an evangelist for a mission called the Angel of Philadelphia and who is as "replete with faith as a fresh-gorged mosquito is with blood." Brother Lemon fails in his "work" of saving souls; he leaves, bewildered and disappointed, but still invincibly armoured with zeal and blind complacency. But Ketteridge buys the Black Christ which had been painted for Brother Lemon's church by the African artist, Danso, and,

> Sometimes, when I am able to see through black and white, until they merge and cease to be separate or apart, I look at those damaged creatures clustering so despairingly hopeful around the Son of Man, and it

seems to me that Brother Lemon, after all, is one of them.   (*The Tomorrow-Tamer*, p. 77)

"The Rain-Child" is narrated by Violet Nedden, who knows that she will always be an outsider in Africa. The passage of years has also made her irrevocably an exile from England, her homeland. She can therefore understand and sometimes help others, like young Ruth and the orphan child, Ayesha, who are fated to be forever homeless:

> Sitting in my garden and looking at the sun on the prickly pear and the poinsettia, I think of that island of grey rain where I must go as a stranger, when the time comes, while others must remain as strangers here.   (*The Tomorrow-Tamer,* p. 133)

The voices of Violet Nedden, of Matthew, and of Will Ketteridge in these three stories are essentially the same voice, with the same tones of self-aware irony, sadness, and sympathy. They are effective in the context of their stories, and they are interesting early experiments in the first-person narrators who are the central—and vastly differentiated—voices of Margaret Laurence's Manawaka novels.

The point and sympathy of each one of the stories narrated in the third person also rests on an outsider—on Adamo, for instance, who has lost everything, in "The Voices of Adamo," or on Kofi, who shifts the beliefs and values of his tribe to the new, technological world of the bridgemen, in "The Tomorrow-Tamer." Because Kofi cannot really enter that world, and does not know how to live safely in it, he is destroyed. In "A Fetish For Love," Constance, the Englishwoman, must learn not to meddle with what she cannot change, and in "The Pure Diamond Man," the point-of-view is, finally, Daniel's, the African whose nephew Tetteh has engaged Hardacre, the Englishman, and the Reverend Timothy Quarshie in the crazy, funny "Casting Nets For The Diamond Fish Game." In "Godman's Master," Godman Pira had not been a part of the living world of men as long as he had been used as a slave-oracle by a fetish priest. He finally finds his manhood and his life's meaning in performing as a "Real Live Oracle" with a travelling troupe of magicians. He is doing freely what he had previously been forced to do by his master:

> "It is not such an easy thing, to find where the laughter is hidden, like gold in the rock. One has to be skilled for this work. The *pirafo* used to be fine jesters, and now, perhaps, again." . . .
> "You have done well," Moses said. "At first I did not see it, but now I see it."
> Godman shrugged.
> "I have known the worst and the worst and the worst," he said, "and yet I live. I fear and fear, and yet I live."
> "No man," Moses said gently, "can do otherwise." . . .
> And Godman Pira waved to Moses and hopped up to take his place with the other performers on the broad and grimy stage.
> (*The Tomorrow-Tamer*, p. 159)

This ending fans out beyond Godman Pira's story to enclose all of us in its irony—"performers on the broad and grimy stage," the world of man.

In "The Perfume Sea," the exotic, funny, and appealing pair, Mr. Archipelago and Doree are drawn together in their loneliness and their sensitivity one to the other. From the inspired Lewis Carroll inconsequence of its beginning, " 'No question of it,' Mr. Archipelago said, delicately snipping a wisp of hair. 'I am flotsam,' " to its shadow-ending, "The sea spray was bitter and salt, but to them it was warm, too," this story is a perfection of the real pushed to the verge of the fantastic, but always stopping just this side of fantasy's border. Archipelago's and Doree's words, appearance, and actions are woven into a story fabric that projects its own truth to our imaginations. In some 8,000 words, these two take on the quality of continuing life that usually attaches itself only to the more spaciously realized characters of a novel.

Margaret Laurence's use of language in this story is delicately effective in producing and sustaining the fine balance of pathos and comedy that constitutes "The Perfume Sea's" tone and its final effect. The resonance of the name "Archipelago" which he himself defines as "flotsam" and "a sea with many islands" is counterpointed throughout to the comedy of his physical presence in the grimy beauty shop, "a fat and frantic wizard, refreshing himself occasionally with Dutch ale." At a deeper level, the pathetic anxieties of Archipelago and Doree, as they anxiously and obediently transform their customers' appearances, resonate against the truth and the depth of their own realities. When they are free of the shop they lead lives of boundless imaginative richness within their house and garden, with their parrots and their perfume:

> Frequently they brought out their perfumes, of which they had a great variety, bottles and flagons of all colours and intricate shapes—crowns and hearts and flowers, diamonded, bubbled, baubled, angular and smooth. The game was to see how many could be identified by smell alone, the vessel masked, before the senses began to flag. Mr. Archipelago did not love the perfumes for themselves alone, nor even for their ability to cover the coarse reek of life. Each one, sniffed like snuff, conjured up for him a throng of waltzing ladies, whirling and spinning eternally on floors of light, their grey gowns swaying, ladies of gentle dust. (*The Tomorrow-Tamer*, p. 34)

But the deepest level of the story, set in benign incongruity to all its tawdry, exotic, comic—and superficial—details, is the extreme sensitivity of their care for each other:

> "For me, the worst would be for you not to have any chance—"

Mr. Archipelago perceived that he had revealed too much. He squirmed and sweated, fearful that she would misunderstand. But when he looked at her, he saw in her eyes not alarm but surprise.

"The necklace and all—" Doree said slowly. "You'd do that—for me?" . . .

"If I wasn't here," she said with a trembling and apologetic laugh, "who'd remind you to put on your hat in the boiling sun? Who'd guess the perfumes with you?"

"I would miss you, of course," he said in a low voice. "I would miss you a great deal."

She turned on him almost angrily. "Don't you think I'd miss you?" she cried. "Don't you know how it would be—for me?"

They stared at each other, wide-eyed, incredulous.   (*The Tomorrow-Tamer*, p. 38)

One story is not enough for Archipelago and Doree, even though all their stories would always, finally, end the same:

The sea spray was bitter and salt, but to them it was warm, too. They watched on the sand their exaggerated shadows, one squat and bulbous, the other bone-slight and clumsily elongated, pigeon and crane. The shadows walked with hands entwined like children who walk through the dark.
                    (*The Tomorrow-Tamer*, p. 49)

Only the final story, "A Gourdful of Glory," is told from the inside by Mamii Ama, who stands for everything positive and hopeful in the newly independent Ghana. Then, when "Free-dom" actually comes, Mamii Ama becomes the outsider herself; she is humiliated by the worldly wisdom of the white woman, who knows that the buses will not automatically give her free rides, and that there can be no sudden transformation to a land flowing with milk and honey for everyone. But Mamii

Ama regains her faith, and in its statement this story—and the book—ends:

> Inspired, Mamii Ama lifted the gourd high above her head, and it seemed to her that she held not a brittle brown calabash, but the world. She held the world in her strong and comforting hands.
> "Free-Dom he come," she cried, half in exaltation, half in longing. "Free-Dom he heah now, dis minute!"   (*The Tomorrow-Tamer*, p. 242)

All of these stories are informed by Margaret Laurence's knowledge of and respect for African history and legend, and by her empathy for the warmth, particularly the maternal warmth, of many of her African characters. "The Tomorrow-Tamer" has, for instance, a quality of authenticity that makes it comparable to Chinua Achebe's *Things Fall Apart*. It communicates the sense of mystery that is so prominent in the lives of a tribal people and that is externalized in their many tales, where it is embodied in a traditional form which does not make the mysterious comprehensible, but does, by its familiarity, help to make the mysterious—and the tragic—bearable. It is her intermittent penetration to the very heart of her subject, along with a constant, brilliant use of more superficial details that gives Margaret Laurence her distinction among non-African writers on Africa. She has a talent for expressing tone and mood through a turn of phrase in conversation or through the placing of a double-edged word or phrase. She has a highly developed feeling for a key dramatic scene that will be the climax of a story's movement and will bring about its swift dénouement. And she has a vivid power of description, of scenes and people given full dimensional quality through details of sight, sound, and smell; and particularly of characters like Mr. Archipelago or Godman Pira who by their vivid eccentricity—their physical but not spiritual grotesquerie—take on life in our imaginations.

Most important, all of these stories are infused and

buoyed up by Margaret Laurence's own enthusiasm about the land of Ghana and its people. Her involvement is illuminated by understanding and a great sympathy, but it is also always underscored by her awareness of herself as irrevocably alien and by the humility that comes from that awareness. Such a position, which involves frustration and regret but which is strongly perceived and held with integrity as a boundary to her understanding, carries over into her stories and shows itself in the qualities of disengagement and detachment that keep them on a middle range of irony, muting their satire on the one end of the scale and their tragedy on the other.

The stories in *The Tomorrow-Tamer* were written for separate publication and over a period of eight years. Collected, a recurring pattern is very evident in them, and finally, in each one a similar response is elicited from the reader, although that response may fluctuate within a considerable range of emotional tone. The child on his journey into experience is, on these stories' deepest level, their central figure, always an exile either spiritually or physically, and often in both senses. Sometimes the character is, in fact, a child, and sometimes he or she is a person who is still in some profound way childlike, like Doree or Constance, Mamii Ama or Adamo, who is Adam—Everyman. The character's appeal is not primarily his innocence; that quality plays an ironic counterpont to his unknowing bravery (in the case of Doree for instance), or to his appalling blindness (in the case of Brother Lemon). The character errs, endures, survives, or sometimes is destroyed; but always there is a dynamic within him that impels him to go on to the end. The essentials of life, Margaret Laurence is always saying, are growth and change and the energy that activates these.

The stories require an active response from the reader, too: not pity, not sympathy, not even love alone, for these can be and often are condescending responses to the predicaments of others; but rather a dynamic kind of "charity" whose components are understanding, love, and a joining, sharing energy. Very often this response, though elicited throughout the story, is made unmistakably and almost didactically clear in its brief epilogue: "The shadows walked with hands entwined like children who walk through the dark;" or "Daniel watched him go, the boy from Gyrakom, rushing away in a burst of sunflowers to seek his fortune in the city streets." Reading them all together one may begin to resist a certain recurrence of technique, while still appreciating the variety of skilled, tightly constructed exercises upon a dominant central theme that *The Tomorrow-Tamer* demonstrates.

This Side Jordan, Margaret Laurence's first novel, was begun in Ghana in 1955, then finished in Vancouver and published in 1960. Like *The Tomorrow-Tamer* stories it came from the background of the Gold Coast and its approaching independence. The situation there, as she saw it in the period between 1952 and 1957, invited a novel of strongly marked pattern, its characters balanced into groups. As was in fact the case in many of the African states of the 1950's, the English in *This Side Jordan* know that their days as masters and managers are numbered; they are, in varying degrees, frightened, resigned, cynical, and resentful. The Africans, in comparable states of hope, dillusion, ignorance, corruption, or cynicism, are in various stages of anticipation and unpreparedness for the actual fact of independence. They must, willy-nilly, be ready to take over problems whose magnitude they cannot even estimate and for whose solution they have neither sufficient training nor sufficient self-confidence.

In *This Side Jordan* the English-centred export-import firm of Allkirk, Moore and Bright employs in its Accra textile branch Johnnie Kestoe, an accountant, whose inexperienced, idealistic wife, Miranda, is expecting a child; Major Bedford Cunningham, whose wife Helen hates and fears Africa for herself and her children; and James Thayer, the branch manager whose only life is with the firm and whose wife Cora clutches with desperate determination at the flimsy status they have managed to achieve in Africa. On the African side, Nathaniel Amegbe, teacher at Jacob Abraham Mensa's "Futura Academy," is caught between his confused, remembered tribal loyalties and those learned at the mission school of his youth; his wife Aya is also expecting a child.

Nathaniel's educated, embittered friend, Victor Edusei, and Charity Donkor, the ignorant village girl Victor takes in bitter consolation for his disillusion with his own people, are set in contrast to Nathaniel's high idealism and Aya's frightened innocence. Various members of Aya's and Nathaniel's families, his fellow teacher, the Highlife boy, Lamptey, and Jacob Mensa himself, give range and variety to the African group. The two groups become involved through Johnnie Kestoe's stubborn, guilty desire for an African woman, through Miranda's well-meaning, misguided, and backfiring friendliness, and through the firm's policy of Africanization, which Johnnie expediently promotes to safeguard his own future, though he is as far from believing in the possibility of its success as are his colleagues. The conflicts bring about no real resolutions, but a kind of limited truce, a working arrangement between the two groups which is really satisfactory to neither. On the personal level, Johnnie and Nathaniel must each make a limited and temporary truce with himself, but each one must recognize and live with his own self-betrayal.

The theme is right, not only for Ghana just before its independence; in its implications—the pressures of inexorable events upon the self-interest and self-doubts of men and women—it is timeless. But in its translation into plot, in Margaret Laurence's first movement from short story to novel, there is an insistence on symmetry and balance in plot and character that in its *origin* is the just impulse to deal fairly and completely with each character, but in its *effect* seems sometimes to be contrivance. After Johnnie and Nathaniel have plunged to their nadirs of self-betrayal and self-distrust and have each achieved some measure of self-awareness, the final chapters, with the evidence of their good intentions and the apportioning of rewards, are almost fussy in their insistence on tying all the threads together. There is a certain forcing of this material within too tight a frame. It is true, as Ciardi says, that the artist takes grave risks when he hacks at the frame; he can, however, either stretch it or pare down his material to fit it. Here there seems to be too much material, with too much neat packaging.

The character of Johnnie Kestoe is strong and memorable, but finally unsatisfying and for a similar reason: too much weight of tragic slum-Irish background has been filled in around the person of a young man who is already entirely believable as we first see him: "Johnnie Kestoe, who didn't like Africans, was dancing the highlife with an African girl." He engages our sympathy from the start by his naïveté, "still being new enough to want to stare at them," by his combination of sensual desire and curiosity, the independence and resentment that prompted him to defy English taboos to dance with Charity, and the honesty in him that admitted his motives, "a disgust that beckoned almost as much as it repelled."

But then he is made to carry the weight of Ireland's mythology with the rhythm of Ireland's speech as well: "The skull of her was more beautiful than the flesh. Fine-shaped as glass, but strong, her bones were the bones of Deirdre, that long-dead queen the poems said no man now can ever dream to be her lover." Then his deprived, loveless background in a London slum is painted along with his searing memories of Mary, his mother, dying through self-inflicted abortion. This in itself is a brilliant piece of writing, with a poignant and unforgettable climax: "From amid the shuttering sobs and the animal paingrunting had come suddenly the clear Irish girlvoice surprised and frightened—'Oh God, my guts won't stop bleeding—what am I going to do at all?' " All this is more than Johnnie Kestoe, in terms of his place and his function in this novel, can carry; here is a surplus of creative, dramatic energy lavished on a character who must finally—if the novel is to succeed—seem a very ordinary man among men, not a tragic hero.

The same tendency towards overemphasis and over-energy, the pen that sometimes etches in acid more easily than in ink and thereby threatens to distort its own composition, can be seen in the entire initial description of the English group. Their fear and their bigotry are real enough and un-derstandable enough without the lines of description that give a witch-like repellance to the pathetic, lost, bird-voiced wife of the manager: "Cora Thayer, who could never sit still, was picking away at her nail varnish with agitated skeletal fingers, pulling away shreds like red scabs." One is reminded here of Margaret Laurence's admission of the prejudice against the English "Imperialists" she first felt in Somaliland. In *The Prophet's Camel Bell*, however, she sketched the amelioration of that prejudice as she comes to know the individuals. Here, in some instances, she has unduly weighted her language against her characters.

These reservations, duly entered against *This Side Jordan*, are, however, far overbalanced by the sureness of tone and the success of technique Margaret Laurence generally achieves in her first novel. Whereas Johnnie Kestoe's background seems overdrawn, Nathaniel Amegbe's is convincing: his conflicts, his achievements, and his failures are rooted in his warring backgrounds and grow organically and inevitably from them. He is the son of Kyerema, the Great Drummer, but he can neither entirely believe in his father's gods nor relinquish them. They still haunt him, because he is also the son of the mission school to which his father sent him: "He believed in the man-God with the bleeding hands and he could not spew that out of himself." Nothing in the book is as convincingly done as Nathaniel's tortured progress towards acceptance of his double heritage, the juxtaposition of his dealings with men and events to the interior monologues in which his past and his people's myths and history struggle to dominate him. His conflict resolves in a believable resolution, even an epiphany:

> In my Father's house are many mansions. A certain
> Drummer dwells in the House of Nyankopon, in that
> City of Many Mansions. I know it now. It is there that
> he dwells, honoured, now and always. It may be that
> I shall never see him again. But let him dwell there in
> peace. Let him understand. No—he will never understand. Let me accept it and leave him in peace.
> (*This Side Jordan*, p. 274).

Then there follows the recognition that Nathaniel, the hero-dreamer, is also the little man of every day, as he engages in his sad, ironic, and supremely human rationalization of having taken bribes from his students:

> How could he return them, anyway? Kumi and Awuletey would not be impressed. They would only think he had gone crazy. They did not expect the gifts back. They had long ago shrugged it off—the luck of the draw. What would he say to them? He would be too embarrassed to say anything to them. They would think he had lost his mind.
>
> He knew if the boys had got the jobs, he would never have considered returning the gifts. Why should he now? A gift was, after all, a gift. Besides, one of the shirts had been worn.
>
> Nathaniel decided to put the whole thing from his mind. He turned his thoughts to the plans he had for next term. He whistled "Akpanga" softly to himself.
>
> And soon the uneasiness passed.
>
> (*This Side Jordan*, p. 275)

The Africans are more believable than the English characters because Margaret Laurence's sympathies were primarily engaged in their portrayals. There is, therefore, an extra element of subtlety and delicacy in their drawing. Victor Edusei binds himself to Charity Donkor, the good-natured whore, because behind his educated cynicism there is a well of human tenderness and a disappointed, unloved child: " 'You won't understand, boy,' he said quietly, 'but I'm fond of that woman. You see, whatever I do, she'll think its great.' " Aya, Nathaniel's wife, is separated from him by her insecurity in the city and her fears of the new ways and new customs. Yet she is loyal enough to bear their son in the dreaded hospital where she was separated from everything familiar; even Jacob Abraham Mensa, a fraudulent and opportunisitic schoolmas-

ter, in his brief appearances becomes recognizable as a complex human being:

> Jacob Abraham was a man of energy and persuasion,
> and he dreamed of glory. . . .
>   "You are a sincere man, Amegbe. Not too
> clever, in some ways, perhaps, but a sincere man
> —that is the thing. You will be Futura's 'kra,' eh?
> How is that?"
>   He laughed uproariously at his joke.
>   Nathaniel tried to laugh, too, but the laughter
> stuck in his throat. He was to be its "kra," then, its
> soul, seeking perfection? Its guide in a new land, its
> ferryman across Jordan. All that, when he did not
> know the way himself?
>   "What does that leave you to be?" he asked.
>   Jacob Abraham chortled appreciatively.
>   "Yes," he said, "just what you are thinking."
>   By the same sacrilegious comparison, Jacob
> Abraham would be the "sunsum" of the school. Its
> personality, filled with self, greedy for life, but with
> an enormous vitality, an enormous will.
>   (*This Side Jordan*, p. 272)

The English characters, though two-dimensional, are
sketched with a skill that often produces the unforgettable
picture—of Thayer, the manager, for instance, faced with
dismissal and retirement:

> As he left, he noticed that James had picked up one of
> the fragments of mammy-cloth once more. The
> Squire was turning it over and over in his hands, and
> his unseeing eyes were fixed on the printed clocks.
>   (*This Side Jordan*, p. 240)

His wife, Cora, pours tea out of a teapot shaped like Anne
Hathaway's cottage. Her tropical bungalow's living room is like
a cheap stage set, a travesty of an English country house. She

collects quarter-yards of beautiful brocades, in pitiful sub-
stitute for the child who had been still-born. The
Cunninghams, too, are adequate as supporting cast: Bedford,
an iron man melting to wax under the pressures of Africa
—"whether he had been accepting the enemies flag, or hand-
ing over his own, his expression would have been the same";
and Helen, who looks like a sloppy, yet magnificent Viking,
and fears the nothingness that awaits them in England even
more than she fears Africa. All of these, though sometimes
brilliantly idiosyncratic as persons, remain essentially
illustrations of types of the colonial English, both paler and
thinner than the African characters. This is particularly so of
Miranda, Johnnie Kestoe's wife. The figure of Constance in "A
Fetish For Love" could well have been a sketch for the character of Miranda. They are really the same person, innocent,
idealistic, and, therefore, potentially, terrifyingly destructive.
But while Constance is adequate to the story in which she finds
her place, the characterization of Miranda is not strong enough
or full enough to make her take her place as a believable
character in the novel.

Margaret Laurence had developed an empathy for Africa
and its people; the deepest springs of her compassion are for
them and the surest parts of her skill are at their service. She
knows Africans in their own setting and she sketches
background in all its sensual detail, not only with its sights and
sounds but with the authenticities of smell and taste added for
their maximum effect. At their best her descriptions realize an
all-dimensional world, vibrant with colours and dense with
sensual effects:

> He walked quickly into the maze of streets, towards
> his home. The air was thick with the pungent smoke
> from charcoal pots and the spiced smell of food being
> cooked in the open, outside every hovel, beside
> every roadside stall. Groundnut stew, bean stew,
> "mme-kwan"—palmnut soup, with the rich sharp
> smell of the palm oil and the salt-and-woodfire smell
> of the smoked fish. The moist yeasty odour of

"kenkey," fermented corn dough, steaming in black
round-bellied cooking pots. The sweet half-cloying
smell of roasting plantains. And over all, the warm
stench of the sea. . . .

The street was a tangle of people. Women in
mammy-cloths of every colour, women straight as
royal palms, balanced effortlessly the wide brass
headpans. A girl breadseller carried on her head a
screened box full of loaves and cakes. Coast men
strolled in African cloth, the bright folds draped casu-
ally around them. Muslims from the north walked tall
and haughty in the loose white trousers and
embroidered robes of their kind. Hausa traders
carried bundles tied up in white and black rough wool
mats. A portly civil servant in khaki shorts wore with
dignity an outdated pith helmet. And everywhere,
there were children, goats and chickens. Vivid,
noisy, chaotic, the life of the street flowed on.

(*This Side Jordan*, p. 44)

Many writers describe with competence, but few of them
attempt total immersion in another sensual world; fewer still
succeed as Margaret Laurence has done. Her ear is naturally
attuned to rhythms and nuances of speech; it was further
trained through working at Somali translations. The precision
of its pickup and transmission of sound patterns is everywhere
evident—subtly so in her characters' speech and sometimes
strongly, deliberately present, as here, through the singing of
the church service:

The preacher raised his arms. He was a small man,
and fat, but when he raised his arms he seemed to
grow enormous, tall as the palms, and his arms
reached out, reached out. The women swayed and
their tears flowed down their singing faces.

"That's salvation, brother! That's salvation! A
man's afraid. He's got fear and he trembles and he

won't come forward. He's afraid to cross that river,
that Jordan. And then he tries. And what happens?
I'll tell you. Yes, I'll tell you! He finds it's easy, easy,
easy! He finds it's easy, for the Lord parts the waters,
and he walks over on dry land. You going to come
over?"

"—Yes, yes!"

"You going to come over?"

"—Yes, yes!"

And they went forward, singing. And the
preacher blessed them and prayed for them.

(*This Side Jordan*, p. 246)

This is a good example of the strongly rhythmic quality of
language that Margaret Laurence, when she wishes, has at her
command and which occurs again and again in all her writings.
It was evident in *The Tomorrow-Tamer* stories, particularly so
in the final lines I have called epilogues. They are aphoristic,
strongly rhythmic, and particularly memorable for that reason.
Her sense of the rhythm of speech patterns and of differences
in those rhythms has always, from the first of her African
writings, been very strong. For that reason her works are
particularly pleasurable to read aloud; some passages do not, in
fact, reveal their richness *until* they are read aloud.

There is in this first novel a splendid liberality, sometimes
a prodigality of talent: situation, drama, place, and personality
strongly felt and vividly expressed; and a wide range of
experience, imaginative, factual, sensual, and sexual,
effectively communicated. The strong narrative thrust propels
the action onward and the reader with it—always enticing him
in the timeless way of the well-told tale to hurry faster, to see
what is coming next. In this first work, the two strongest
characters are men. The character of Johnnie Kestoe, though
overburdened for his particular role in this particular novel,
shows her potential for the strong "outsider" figure which has
been central to all her Manawaka novels in the persons of both
women and men. And certainly the figures of Bram Shipley,

Christy Logan, and Jules Tonnerre have developed a potential for male characterization that was already plainly marked in her drawing of Johnnie Kestoe.

Finally, the foundation strength of *This Side Jordan*, as well as of *The Tomorrow-Tamer*, a substructure to everything else in either work, is Margaret Laurence's passionate insistence on the dignity of the individual. This is the solid inner drumbeat of the novel. During the characters' best moments they are in time with it; during their worst moments they are off-beat. But the beat itself is always there, never faltering or compromising, and always dynamic. It remains within and behind the action, and its energy, its embodiment in her fiction, pushes the reader beyond simple acquiescence to an answering energy of affirmation.

These works Margaret Laurence wrote out of her experience of Africa, but in them she by no means exhausted the effects of Africa's impact on her. The theme of exile and the question "where is home?"; feelings about tribalism and community, about our exploiting of one another, about the ambivalence of tragic failures and joyous victories: all these have become strands in the fabric of all her fiction. And basic to all her work since has been her astonished wonder at the indomitable vitality and endurance of the spirit of man. Nathaniel Amegbe, caught between a past he cannot exorcise and a present he cannot understand, remembers his boyhood, the beauty of the forest and its accompaniment, fear:

> When I was a boy on my father's farm, the forest was peopled with a million ghosts, a million gods. Stone and tree and root, a million eyes. I was not brave. I was slight and small for my age, and my mother had protected me too much. I was not brave. Was any-one? (*This Side Jordan*, p. 105)

The Somalis and the Ghanaians had seemed unbelievably brave to Margaret Laurence and she had written testimony to their spirit. She has built on the same core of wonder and affirmation throughout her subsequent work.

Back in Vancouver from 1957 to 1962 she also served the final part of her apprenticeship to writing as a profession. She was a full-time wife and mother and a part-time writer, the hours of her work squeezed in meagrely—and guiltily. As Willa Cather wrote in *The Song of the Lark*, "Every artist makes himself born. It is very much harder than the other time, and longer." During these years Margaret Laurence gradually came to accept herself as a writer and to know that she must do her work. Writing was her gift and vocation, both joy and doom. The decisions involved in her acceptance were not made without struggle and pain. She and Jack Laurence finally separated and she and the children went to England.

Africa had been the goal of her first departure and its experiences had released and quickened her talent. Practically, the goal of this second departure was, simply, London. She felt, as have so many other writers, the lure of the large metropolitan literary centre, and she hoped to make connections there with her tribe, the writers of the world. In another and more important way it was necessary for Margaret Laurence to detach herself from Canada for one more period of her life. She was ready to write about Manawaka now, but she still needed distance to see it clearly.

FOUR

The Stone Angel

I cried. And had not thought till then
that there was such a bright salvation in a tear;
my mother had not told me only faith
could sail a sea of glass and fear.

> Edward Brathwaite. "The Cracked Mother"
> *Islands*.

If *This Side Jordan* sometimes staggered beneath the accumulated force of Margaret Laurence's writing talents, her second novel, *The Stone Angel*, provided balance and focus for them. The character of Hagar Shipley had been in her mind for a long time: "I don't think I have ever written anything in which the main character hasn't been in my mind for at least several years, sometimes many years." The actual writing of the first draft of *The Stone Angel* occurred in Vancouver in 1961 and the beginning of 1962. In a very considerable sense her fictional realization of Hagar Shipley was both tribute and memorial to the two persons who had most deeply marked her youth: her tough and terrifying grandfather, John Simpson, who had died in 1953, and beloved step-mother, Margaret Simpson Wemyss, who had died in 1957.

The novel was also written during the time when her talent was forcing its choice upon her. When she and the children moved to England its first draft was finished; after a year's interval, distanced and detached from her Canadian background, she rewrote the novel. *The Stone Angel* was published in England, America, and Canada in 1964.

Hagar Shipley not only could bear, but also demanded Margaret Laurence's particular powers at their fullest play. She tells us her story in her own compelling voice and in so doing she brings her own life and, for the first time, the town of Manawaka vividly and unforgettably into being. Like her biblical namesake, Hagar wanders in a wilderness, and like the stone angel in the Manawaka cemetery, "she was doubly blind, not only stone but unendowed with even a pretense of sight." At ninety, when the book begins, she is grotesque with the fat ugliness of her old age, and her nature is twisted and distorted by the self-willed tragedies of her life. She is a proud, bitter, sick, and frightened old woman, with a whip-lash tongue to cut and mock, even at herself. Above all, she is "rampant with memory"; and she is still, and desperately, rampant with life. We share in her last short and bitter struggle to maintain her independence; more important, we share in her halting, unwilling, rebellious journey towards self-knowledge and, finally, a limited peace.

The actual events of the novel take place over a short time-span—two, perhaps three weeks. But in the sharp struggle of her last days, Hagar recalls, defends, questions, and finally accepts and understands all the events and the feelings that have been important to her in her ninety years. She moves from the present to the past and back again with an ease that is completely familiar to those who have listened to and watched the old. The anxiety lest she confuse past and present and so prove herself to be as "queer" and incapable as her son and daughter-in-law think her to be is familiar too.

Hagar lives with her son Marvin and his wife Doris, both of them well into their sixties, in a house in Vancouver which she worked for and bought; the house is the sum of all her achievement—and her *only* achievement has been in the gathering together of a few things, never in her relationships with people. The house's familiarity, its possessions, and the tokens it holds from her past—the oak chair that belonged to her father, Jason Currie, and the cut-glass decanter, her wed-

ding gift from Bram Shipley—these are the only solid
evidences of identity that Hagar now possesses:

> My shreds and remnants of years are scattered
> through it visibly in lamps and vases, the needle-
> point fire bench, the heavy oak chair from the Ship-
> ley place, the china cabinet and walnut sideboard
> from my father's house. There'd not be room for
> these in some cramped apartment. We'd have to put
> them into storage, or sell them. I don't want that. I
> couldn't leave them. If I am not somehow contained
> in them and in this house, something of all change
> caught and fixed here, eternal enough for my
> purposes, then I do not know where I am to be found
> at all.   (*The Stone Angel*, p. 36)

She is ill, stabbed with a pain under her ribs that grips her
without warning; grotesquely fat and uncertain on her feet;
sometimes incontinent; unable to care for herself and yet
resentful of Doris and Marvin's fussy care and bumbling concern; completely at the mercy of her physical debility and
revolted at its manifestations, and yet merciless towards those
who try to help her. Above all, she is still capable of merciless
honesty towards herself:

> I give a sideways glance at the mirror, and see a
> puffed face purpled with veins as though someone
> had scribbled over the skin with an indelible pencil.
> The skin itself is the silverish white of the creatures
> one fancies must live under the sea where the sun
> never reaches. Below the eyes the shadows bloom as
> though two soft black petals had been stuck there.
> The hair which should by rights be black is yellowed
> white, like damask stored too long in a damp
> basement.
>   Well, Hagar Shipley, you are a sight for sore
> eyes, all right.   (*The Stone Angel*, p. 79)

Hagar's rebellious pride still refuses to accommodate to the fact of her old age, or to the fact that the processes of time are irreversible, and that she must face death, probably soon. As she is repellent physically, especially to herself, she is just as ugly in her cruelty toward Doris—"that Doris, . . . puffing and sighing like a sow in labour." She is blind and mistaken in her judgement of Marvin—"there is a boy who never gets upset, not even at what happened to his own brother." But nevertheless she compels a grudging admiration, an unflagging interest, and the tension of partisanship one always accords the gallant fighter fated to lose. Only her body has aged; her spirit is indomitably young, tough, and brave. "I never got used to a single thing," she says, and her unchanging dark eyes symbolize the stubborn, flaming vitality that still burns in her:

> For when I look in my mirror and beyond the changing shell that houses me, I see the eyes of Hagar Currie, the same dark eyes as when I first began to remember and to notice myself. . . . The eyes change least of all. (*The Stone Angel*, p. 38)

The sensual being does not change much either, and Hagar at ninety is still delighted by her senses' gratifications: in fact, she is often greedy for them. She loves colour: the back-garden yellow with forsythia, or her lilac silk dress, "a real silk, mine, spun by worms in China, feeding upon the mulberry leaves." Doris' food she grudgingly admires and heartily enjoys, whatever the cost to her tired digestive system:

> I eat well. My appetite is usually very good. I have always believed there could not be much wrong with a person if they ate well. Doris has done a roast of beef, and she gives me the inner slices, knowing I like it rare, the meat a faint, brownish pink. She makes good gravy, to give her her due. It's never lumpy, always a silken brown. For dessert we have

> peach pie, and I have two helpings. Her crust's a little
> richer than I used to make, and not so flaky but quite
> tasty nonetheless.　　　　　(*The Stone Angel*, p. 67)

Colours, sounds, and smells come to her as vividly as ever
they did, from her past and from her present, and the old
woman is still almost miraculously identifiable as the same
Hagar who began to enjoy sex very soon after her marriage,
though she was too proud to let Bram, her husband, know it.
When she had finally left Manawaka and Bram,

> I'd waken, sometimes, out of a half sleep and turn to
> him and find he wasn't beside me, and then I'd be
> filled with such a bitter emptiness it seemed the
> whole of night must be within me and not around or
> outside at all. There were times when I'd have
> returned to him, just for that.
> 　　　　　　　　　　　　(*The Stone Angel*, p. 160)

It is an enormous affirmation of living and feeling that
Hagar makes, and to its energy we cannot help responding as
children, reassured. Nor can we help a response compounded
of pity and wonder at her stubborn gallantry, and at the pathos
and irony of a recurrent double-exposure image of
Hagar—old, ugly, chained, and earth-bound by her physical
disintegration, and young, vivid, strong, and untamed as a
hawk:

> Then I fall. . . . I gasp and flounder like a fish on the
> slimed boards of a dock. . . .
> 　　Then, terribly, I perceive the tears, my own
> they must be although they have sprung so unbidden
> I feel they are like the incontinent wetness of the
> infirm. Trickling, they taunt down my face. They are
> no tears of mine, in front of her. I dismiss them,
> blaspheme against them—let them be gone. But I
> have not spoken, and they are still there.
> 　　　　　　　　　　　　(*The Stone Angel*, p. 31)

The pathos of such a passage is unforgettably heightened by Hagar's indomitable spirit and by her bewildered regret for the loss of the youth and strength that once matched her spirit:

> Yet now I feel that if I were to walk carefully up to my room, approach the mirror softly, take it by surprise, I would see there again that Hagar with the shining hair, the dark-maned colt off to the training ring, the young ladies' academy in Toronto.
>
> (*The Stone Angel*, p. 42)

The story moves forward on two levels. The present carries Hagar's determination to avoid Silverthreads, the nursing-home, to its climax in her panic flight from Vancouver to a deserted fish-cannery up the coast, and from there, after a hidden and healing two days, to a final hospital bed. Complementary to it, and called up from her memory by the present's various moments, moves the past, "the incommunicable years," blasted by the pride that ruined Hagar's marriage and blinded her to the natures and the needs of her husband and her two sons. And finally when the past and the present have fused in the cannery and all the errors have been laid bare and admitted, there is still time in the short time left to Hagar for her to make some signal act of restitution:

> I lie here and try to recall something truly free that I've done in ninety years. I can think of only two acts that might be so, both recent. One was a joke—yet a joke only as all victories are, the paraphernalia being unequal to the event's reach. The other was a lie—yet not a lie, for it was spoken at least and at last with what may perhaps be a kind of love.
>
> (*The Stone Angel*, p. 307)

Sometimes Hagar moves between present and past with apparent inconsequence of connection; more often the past is evoked for her by some thought, some sight or sound in the present. Then again, she will be jolted out of reverie in the past by some pressure from the present, a sound or a physical sensation that impinges on the reverie. Consequently the book falls into a pattern of parallel scenes, present and past juxtaposed, each moving toward a climactic fusing in the deserted cannery and then levelling off in the hospital. Such a symmetry of pattern might, less skilfully done, less believably evoked, have forced an unconvincing, brittle rigidity upon the novel.

In "Gadgetry or Growing? . . Form and Voice in the Novel," a lecture given at the University of Toronto in 1969, Margaret Laurence questioned and discussed her parallel structuring of *The Stone Angel*:

> I decided I would have to write it in the present tense, with flashbacks in the past tense. This method seemed a little rigid, but I was dealing with a very rigid character. I did not really like the flashback method much, but I could not discover any alternative which would convey the quality and events of Hagar's long past. In a sense, I think this method works not too badly in *The Stone Angel* simply because Hagar *is* so old, *is* living largely in her past, does—like many old people—remember the distant past better than the present.

She had worked with the notion of having Hagar's memories occur haphazardly, but had rejected this technique as being too confusing for the reader:

> I am still not sure that I decided the right way when I decided to place Hagar's memories in chronological order. One can say that the method I chose diminishes the novel's resemblance to life, but on the other hand, writing—however consciously unordered its method—is never as disorderly as life. Art, in fact, is never life. It is never as paradoxical, chaotic, complex or as alive as life.

The Stone Angel's effect and its credibility, the degree of illusion of life that it gives, essentially depend upon the reader's acceptance of Hagar. The reader's initial suspension of disbelief gradually grows into a temporary subordination of self to this woman whose fictional reality is so forceful. Hagar's reality is evidence of Margaret Laurence's meaning when she says, "I think that fiction is truer than fact," and her authenticity is assured by the authenticity of her voice. Margaret Laurence has spoken of her "enormous conviction of the authenticity of Hagar's voice" as she wrote the novel, and of her pleasure in rediscovering an idiom she had not known she remembered, the idiom of her grandparents. Any questions about a forced tidiness of form are hushed as Hagar takes shape and authority; this, we are convinced, is the way she would speak and remember, strongly biased in all her judgements, forcing order on her own mind as she had tried always to force her own order on all those around her.

Then, too, the building up of a story scene by scene is a technique that Margaret Laurence had practised well and often in her short stories. Well done, the technique is brilliantly effective, striking the reader with the impact of a film; such a work is first a sensuous, predominantly visual experience and then an emotional one. The insights and the perceptions are built on a base that is as directly a sense-communication as words can afford, with the over-layers of suggestion and meaning that *only* words can supply. Nothing, for instance, could more firmly establish Hagar as a woman worth listening to than the opening paragraphs of the book:

> Above the town, on the hill brow, the stone angel used to stand. I wonder if she stands there yet, in memory of her who relinquished her feeble ghost as I gained my stubborn one, my mother's angel that my father bought in pride to mark her bones and proclaim his dynasty, as he fancied, forever and a day. . . .
>
> In summer the cemetery was rich and thick

as syrup with the funeral-parlour perfume of the
planted peonies, dark crimson and wallpaper pink,
the pompous blossoms hanging leadenly, too heavy
for their light stems, bowed down with the weight of
themselves and the weight of the rain, infested with
upstart ants that sauntered through the plush petals
as though to the manner born.

I used to walk there often when I was a girl.
There could not have been many places to walk prim-
ly in those days, on paths, where white kid boots and
dangling skirts would not be torn by thistles or put in
unseemly disarray. How anxious I was to be neat and
orderly, imagining life had been created only to
celebrate tidiness, like prissy Pippa as she passed.
But sometimes through the hot rush of disrespectful
wind that shook the scrub oak and the coarse
couchgrass encroaching upon the dutifully cared-for
habitations of the dead, the scent of the cowslips
would rise momentarily. They were tough-rooted,
these wild and gaudy flowers, and although they
were held back at the cemetery's edge, torn out by
loving relatives determined to keep the plots clear
and clearly civilized, for a second or two a person
walking there could catch the faint, musky, dust-
tinged smell of things that grew untended and had
grown always, before the portly peonies and the
angels with rigid wings, when the prairie bluffs were
walked through only by Cree with enigmatic faces
and greasy hair.

Now I am rampant with memory.

(*The Stone Angel*, pp. 3-5)

Hagar's voice speaks with a ground-tone of irony that is
sustained in the tightest of tensions throughout the entire
work. Her irony ranges from bitter self-mockery and cruel
mockery of others through laughter that usually has a bitter
flavour to a final wondering acceptance of paradox, sometimes
funny, sometimes tragic, as the basic element for strength
and for weakness in the fabric of life. "Pride was my

wilderness"—strength was my weakness—is Hagar's moment of truth. Hagar's powerful voice in all its range of irony is achieved through a densely patterned prose-fabric of images that are authentic to her time and place and to the idioms, the attitudes—and the clichés—of her generation.*

Hagar is herself a ruined angel in the destructive energy of her pride. She is also, in her perceptions, a poet, her imagination rampaging to match her memory, making patterns of reality, of lost bright dreams, and of gothic darkness out of all that she has known. And you, the reader, are caught and held by the sound of her voice, if you are drawn to the first picture of that stone angel, or to the smell of those peonies; if you recognize some of the truth of your own voice in that balance of self-indulgence and self-mockery, and an authenticity of memory in those thickly clustering images and in the lines that are as strongly marked in their rhythm as lines of poetry. Such a quick establishment of Hagar was necessary if the novel was to succeed; her appeal is firmly set in two-and-a-half pages, and it continues to overbalance her minimal reality as a bad-tempered, ugly old woman, and to carry us along by its continuing vigour.

Hagar lived in battle, pitted against everyone who came close to her and, tragically, she betrayed them all—her father, her brothers, her husband, and her sons. Even for John, the younger son in whom she placed all her hopes, her love was blind and ultimately destructive. The pride that destroyed her relations with others is established in the first paragraph of her novel as her father's error also; Jason Currie had directed his enormous will towards "proclaiming his dynasty" and "getting ahead" in the microcosmic world of Manawaka where he had come as a pioneer. Hagar sees her mother's monument as a symbol of her father's place in the town and of his pride:

> I think now she must have been carved in that distant
> sun by stone masons who were the cynical
> descendants of Bernini, gouging out her like by the

---

*Bernice Lever of York University is engaged in a study of "Nature Imagery in the Manawaka Works of Margaret Laurence."

score, gauging with admirable accuracy the needs of
fledgling pharaohs in an uncouth land.

(The Stone Angel, p. 3)

Hagar's bitter sneer at "fledgling pharaohs in an uncouth land"
etches in acid the worst elements of Manawaka—the rawness
of the land and the mean and material ambitions of its leaders.
Moreover, the word "pharaohs," in the cluster of its dark
connotation, of power, wealth, and death, casts its shadows
forward over Hagar's story.

Hagar took and treasured the ancient battle-cry of the
Currie clan, "Gainsay Who Dare," but ironically, her "daring"
was the destructive defiance of her marriage to Bram Shipley,
against her father, against the town which she thought she
despised and very shortly against Bram himself. She thought
her son, John, was heir to the old spirit of the battle-cry, but
she finally betrayed him in the name of "appearances," "commonsense," and "getting ahead." John died, as did Arlene
Simmons whom he loved; but in a stupid, pointless, drunken
dare, in hopeless rebellion against a combination of Depression, poverty, and hostile circumstances that Hagar had par-
tially contrived.

Throughout the novel a world of dualities is constantly
with us, in the juxtaposition of the physical Hagars, young and
old, and also in the contrast between a Hagar who is supported
and ennobled by her enduring pride and the same Hagar,
ruined by it. We are constantly made aware of the clashing of
appearances and realities: Hagar as she thinks she is and as she
really is; Hagar as she reads her motives in the past and as they
seem to us; Marvin as she sees him and as we gradually com-
prehend him to be; Doris, often intolerable by Hagar's
standards and by ours, but just as often a tired, middle-aged
woman who loves her husband enough to bear with an impossible mother-in-law. Bram Shipley takes shape with
particular reality. As the story progresses, he moves into focus
from shadow—the man the young Hagar thought she saw and
could change—to substance—the man he really was, trapped
in his own nature as Hagar was in hers. "His banner over me

was love," she says, and more and more in her recollections of
him there is a humble regret and bewilderment that so much
could have been thrown away to the ruin of them both.

There are also many vignettes of the characters who are on
the verges of Hagar's self-prison: her doctor, the matron of
Silverthreads, Doris' clergyman, Mr. Troy, Mrs. Steiner,
whom she meets at the nursing home, and the companions of
her final hospital days. All of these people, briefly
encountered, still give a sense of their entirety, of real lives
impinging briefly, with varying affects, upon Hagar's. One of
them, Murray F. Lees, is her companion in her desperate,
fish-cannery refuge; his function is analogous to the Fool's in
King Lear's extremity of agony on the heath. Lees lives with
the tragedy of his son's death; the child was burned to death in
a fire at his home, while his parents were praying at the
Redeemer's Advocates' Tabernacle for a revelation about the
coming of the New Kingdom. From time to time he escapes
with a jug of wine. He, his wine, and his compulsive telling of
his story propel Hagar to the final stages of her story and her
only possible escape from her guilt and self-torment: her facing
and confessing that part of her life she had always been unable
to confess—her responsibility in John's death. Murray Lees is
more than an agent for her release, however; his identity
remains autonomous, with the grotesque and pitiful reality of a
person who astonishingly has suddenly emerged from behind
the lines of a sordid, pathetic newspaper story.

The suspense generated by Hagar's remembering journey
through her life and its climax in her telling of the story of
John's death is temporarily satisfied by her release into a
confusion of mind. Only later in the hospital, however, does
Hagar realize that she has been truly freed. Her mind is
perfectly clear again and her moment of revelation and self-
knowledge comes when Mr. Troy, the clergyman whom she
had despised, sings "Old Hundred," the hymn she had wanted
to hear:

I would have wished it. This knowing comes upon me
so forcefully, so shatteringly, and with such a

bitterness as I have never felt before. I must always, always, have wanted that—simply to rejoice. How is it I never could? I know, I know. How long have I known? Or have I always known, in some far crevice of my heart, some cave too deeply buried, too concealed? Every good joy I might have held, in my man or any child of mine or even the plain light of morning, of walking the earth, all were forced to a standstill by some brake of proper appearances—oh, proper to whom? When did I ever speak the heart's truth?

Pride was my wilderness, and the demon that led me there was fear. I was alone, never anything else, and never free, for I carried my chains within me, and they spread out from me and shackled all I touched.   (*The Stone Angel*, p. 292)

The Stone Angel does not end in this revelation, though it is Hagar's moment of truth and, for the reader, the moment of catharsis. In the short time left before her story ends, there is time and opportunity for Hagar to make some steps towards the restitution she needs to make, and to accept the evidence of love she has always wanted. She can let down her defences towards Marvin and give him the assurance he has always needed:

Now it seems to me he is truly Jacob, gripping with all his strength, and bargaining. *I will not let thee go, except thou bless me.* And I see I am thus strangely cast, and perhaps have been so from the beginning, and can only release myself by releasing him.

It's in my mind to ask his pardon, but that's not what he wants from me.

"You've not been cranky, Marvin. You've been good to me, always. A better son than John."

The dead don't bear a grudge nor seek a blessing. The dead don't rest uneasy. Only the living.

Marvin, looking at me from anxious elderly eyes, believes me. It doesn't occur to him that a person in my place would ever lie. (*The Stone Angel*, p. 304)

Marvin cannot rise above the hackneyed commonplace in speech, but Hagar, who always despised his inarticulateness as much as she hated his father's vulgarity of language, can now see through the words to the spirit behind them. When she overhears him outside in the corridor speaking of her, she is, at last, able to give thanks:

A pause, and then Marvin replies.
"She's a holy terror," he says.
Listening, I feel like it is more than I could now reasonably have expected out of life, for he has spoken with such anger and such tenderness.
(*The Stone Angel*, p. 304)

A strongly marked sacramental pattern moves with benign irony through *The Stone Angel*. The spirit of the religion that Hagar has known since a child only in the emptiness of its forms takes her from a terrible sense of sin and guilt through repentance and confession, towards freedom, and on to the simple but signal acts of restitution that finally constitute her brief and limited temporal freedom. She still considers herself "unregenerate," in the guilt-haunted terminology of her Calvinist heritage. But the pattern culminates as Hagar does lose her life to find it, in the splendid, strongly marked symbolism of the final lines—a fighting, dying, stubborn old woman—a glass of water, the cup of life, the grace of God:

I wrest from her the glass, full of water to be had for the taking. I hold it in my own hands. There. There.
And then— (*The Stone Angel*, p. 308)

Life does not often offer us such a rounded completeness of pattern, though life does most strangely answer the demands of the will. Fortunately there is art, opening up glimpses of the possible whole, burning away fear and pity to make places for acceptance, charity, and the endurance to go on.

Symbolically Hagar is, of course, a wanderer in the wilderness through her own wilfulness, like the biblical Hagar. She is the second wife of Bram Shipley, and she resents and despises the memory of the first one as the biblical Hagar resented Sarah, Abraham's wife. Bram Shipley, with his failed farm, is no patriarch; though sadly and ironically, he wishes to be one and hopes their first child will be a boy:

> "It would be somebody to leave the place to," he said.
> I saw then with amazement that he wanted his dynasty no less than my father had.
>
> (*The Stone Angel*, p. 101)

Hagar flees Bram and the farm and lives self-exiled with her son John, who does grow up to be an Ishmael, an outsider. Hagar is also "The Stone Angel," whose image presides magnificently over the novel as its blind presence presides over the town of Manawaka—but Hagar's eyes are finally opened and, in the end, she sees. The fish-cannery refuge and the seagull who comes there have a symbolic resonance that links them to the Christian sacramental pattern of the whole work. Their primary effectiveness, however, is their simple, convincing reality of place and incident.

Everywhere in the book, the reality of place and time, the authenticity of incident and mood, are made completely convincing by the vitality of Hagar's voice and its vividness in calling up the world she experiences now and her other worlds, remembered. It is no compliment to a novel as a work of art to say that it might well be used as a textbook in geriatrics; or that its last pages are a perfect casebook on both the sad reassurances and the maddening frustrations of a patient in hospital. To say these things of *The Stone Angel* does, however, give recognition to one facet of the book: Margaret Laurence handles a myriad of detail with the absolute assurance and authority that E. J. Pratt evinced for the sea and ships, or Hugh MacLennan for the Halifax explosion, or Gabrielle Roy for the sights and sounds of Montreal in the thirties. Margaret Laurence has said of her writing that she wants to put down on paper what everyone knows but nobody has thought of saying—truth of detail and wealth of detail play a large part in her success.

The smell of peonies in a graveyard, the look of forsythia in bloom, the smell of Fels Naptha soap in a freshly scrubbed farm kitchen, or that same kitchen with its worn and creaking T. Eaton couch and its table oilcloth thick with grease and flies, the failed-farm look of the Shipley place, "the yard muddy and puddled with yellow ammonia pools where the horses emptied themselves," the tough, fragile-looking lilacs in that same yard, their scent "a seasonal mercy": each of these, like scores of others, brings with it or brings to our consciousness a surprised, confirming flash of recognition—"this is exactly how it is."

Hagar is a tragic figure, a stone angel whose eyes learn to see just before it is too late; but more than that she is real, with an energy of presence that bursts the frame it is held in to communicate its power, its pathos, and its vitality directly, like a blow or a sharp cry. Like the stone angel in the Manawaka cemetery, a symbol of pride and not of love, and Deg-Der, the cannibal queen in *A Tree For Poverty*, Hagar is a Grotesque as her story begins. She is distorted physically and spiritually, a being monstrous without its appropriate spirit; only through her agony of self-recognition does she moderate from enormity to humanity. To confront her is to recognize, with stunning impact, her presence in our past, in our present—and in ourselves.

George Eliot spoke of the process of writing a novel as a movement toward conceiving "with that directness which is no longer reflection but feeling—an idea wrought back to the directness of sense." In her conception of Hagar and in her telling of Hagar's story, Margaret Laurence has done just that, and her subject required the particular directness of sensual impression which she commands most successfully. The character of Hagar exploited a talent that brought to her creation an empathy and a flamboyant vigour that completely answered the requirements of Hagar's total reality.

Hagar's banner compounds pride with strength, like the Currie war cry "Gainsay Who Dare!" In this she is a symbol of Manawaka itself, whose powerful, corporate personality is mapped out for us in *The Stone Angel*. Jason Currie and his like were proud, strong, "God-fearing" men who performed feats of endurance in the service of their goals of personal success and social progress. Their pride sustained them, but it was a two-edged sword. Its cost was reckoned in terms of losses they did not see, failures in humanity whose effects were built into the generations after them.

FIVE

A Jest of God

My mother said I'd be alone
And when I cried (she said)
I'd be Columbus of my ships
And sail the garden round
The tears that fell into my hand.

> Edward Brathwaite, "The Cracked Mother"
> *Islands.*

With the story of Hagar, Margaret Laurence found the way to go back to Manawaka, to the place of her own past and her own people which as a child she had named as the home of the pioneers, the "Pillars of the Nation." Since *The Stone Angel*, her works have been illuminations of various facets of her perceptions about that place and its people. From the way in which each work makes a totally harmonious part of the whole cycle of the Manawaka works, one recognizes an entire pattern that was present, complete, from the beginning. Each novel and story since *The Stone Angel* has extracted certain strands of the pattern as they came together in the lives of her characters, set them down, and made them plain. *The Stone Angel, A Jest of God, A Bird in the House,* and *The Fire-Dwellers* are segments of a whole, not stations in a continuum; *The Diviners* completes the pattern and closes the circle. *A Jest of God,* the story of Rachel Cameron's ordeal through a summer in Manawaka in the 1960's, was written at Elm cottage, Margaret

77

Laurence's house in Buckinghamshire, England, in 1964 and 1965, and published in 1966.

Both Hagar and Rachel had been in her mind for many years before Margaret Laurence wrote their stories: "The difficulty always seems to me that I know far too much about any character, and cannot possibly get it across as I would like to be able to do." The power and the tragedy of Hagar Shipley had the brilliance of a solar explosion and, for many readers, a somewhat comparable impact. When she turned to Rachel, Margaret Laurence was writing of a character radically different, one who, in contrast to Hagar, required a palette in shades of gray. Rachel Cameron, daughter of Niall Cameron, an undertaker in Manawaka, is a spinster school teacher. She lives in uneasy misery with her widowed mother, locked within her own fears and inhibitions, her strength constantly sapped by a self-debasing humility as destructive as Hagar's pride and, as one is finally led to perceive it, the mirror image of that pride. Rachel is desperate with the need to reach out and touch some life outside her own, and yet she is bound by the negative imperatives that make up her own emotional life: the chafing ties of duty to her mother, the frustration of her surrogate maternal affection for young James Doherty whom she teaches, and the guilt of her obsessive sexual fantasies. The "brake of proper appearances," which Hagar finally acknowledged as her demon, regulates Rachel's actions and makes a tormenting guilt-ridden see-saw of her thoughts. She is full of fear of everything within her claustrophobic circle of hell, and of anything outside of it.

Mrs. Cameron, Rachel's mother, is an egocentric hypchondriac bound to her fears and her pills. Her pleasures in life are the small vanities of high heels, fussy blue-rinsed curls, and bridge parties. These and the dependence and servitude of her daughter are all she has, and to them she clings with every ploy that cunning, born of self-indulgence and a real and desperate need, can suggest. Rachel also is neurotic and egocentric; emotionally, she and her mother are both children, each unwilling and unable to grow up and leave the other free, each battening on the weakness of the other.

In the first paragraphs of *The Stone Angel*, arrogant old Hagar recalls a graveyard angel,

> pointing with ecstatic leer to an inscription. I remember that inscription because we used to laugh at it when the stone was first placed there.

> *Rest in peace.*
> *From toil, surcease.*
> *Regina Weese.*
> *1886*

> So much for sad Regina, now forgotten in Manawaka—as I, Hagar, am doubtless forgotten. And yet I always felt she had only herself to blame, for she was a flimsy, gutless creature, bland as egg custard, caring with martyred devotion for an ungrateful foxvoiced mother year in and year out.
>
> *(The Stone Angel*, p. 4)

Here, in Rachel, is Regina resuscitated, the cruelly caricatured "old maid" humanized and dignified, the author's insistent voice saying behind Rachel's own, "this is a person, certainly flimsy and perhaps gutless, no heroics, no Promethean pride here, but a living human being, capable of growth and demanding respect. Attention must be paid."

Rachel is not brave—neither defiantly so, as Hagar, nor unconsciously, unknowingly so, as Adamo and Kofi in the African stories. Consequently, she lacks the immediate appeal of these characters. On the contrary, she is plummeted and buffeted by every fear she conjures up, and yet even her range of fearing is narrow. Her will is a negligible force; she does things, makes decisions, hardly at all by choice, simply through desperation, or in the hopeless rut of lethargy that abdicates action for routine. Yet even so, she is pushed and battered—and pushes and batters herself—into growth, decision, and a limited, but for her, an enormous victory.

Rachel requires enormous authorial tact and skill to

engage and hold, and then to impel, our sympathy and respect. As different from Hagar as Prufrock is from Lear, she wavers on the brink of hysteria, and her voice, through the book's first three chapters, is like one long, barely controlled scream. Like Hagar, Rachel speaks to us in the first person. Technically, this novel's success, as *The Stone Angel*'s, depends upon the immediate involving of the reader in the sound of her voice and the dimensions of her imagination. She speaks first as she stands looking out the window of her Grade Two classroom at the children in the school yard. She is walled in by glass from even the illusion of freedom that their play presents, and she is desperately afraid of her own shadow-fears and fantasies. The first page and a half of the book tell us everything basic to our understanding of Rachel's tormented, self-doubting mind and her present state of near-hysteria:

> *The wind blows low, the wind blows high*
> *The snow comes falling from the sky,*
> *Rachel Cameron says she'll die*
> *For the want of the golden city.*
> *She is handsome, she is pretty,*
> *She is the queen of the golden city—*

They are not actually chanting my name, of course. I only hear it that way from where I am watching at the classroom window, because I remember myself skipping rope to that song when I was about the age of the little girls out there now. Twenty-seven years ago, which seems impossible, and myself seven, but the same brown brick building, only a new wing added and the place smartened up. It would certainly have surprised me then to know I'd end up here, in this room, no longer the one who was scared of not pleasing, but the thin giant She behind the desk at the front. . . .

> *Spanish dancers, turn around,*
> *Spanish dancers, get out of this town.*

People forget the songs, later on, but the knowledge
of them must be passed like a secret language from
child to child—how far back? . . .

> *Nebuchadnezzar, King of the Jews,*
> *Sold his wife for a pair of shoes.*

I can imagine that one going back and back, through
time and languages. Chanted in Latin, maybe, the
same high sing-song voices, smug little Roman girls
safe inside some villa in Gaul or Britain, skipping
rope on a mosaic courtyard, not knowing the blue-
painted dogmen were snarling outside the walls,
stealthily learning. There. I am doing it again. This
must stop. It isn't good for me. Whenever I find
myself thinking in a brooding way, I must simply turn
it off and think of something else. God forbid that I
should turn into an eccentric.   (*A Jest of God*, pp. 1-2)

We are held initially by the sadness of Rachel's voice and by the
spread of her imagination. Every adult recognizes her dream
and its loss, and we become engaged in sympathy for her by the
gap between her young, dream-self, "Queen of the Golden
City," and her thirty-four-year-old reality, shut in behind her
window, looking out and worrying about becoming an
eccentric spinster, that stereotyped butt of cruel laughter. In
Rachel's Manawaka, "proper appearances" are strictly defined
and do not include any hint of strangeness: *"Spanish dancers,
turn around, Spanish dancers get out of town."* As with Hagar,
whose voice quickly reaches back through time to the Pharaohs, so Rachel's voice moves away from her own problems
through time, first compelling and then, as the book goes on,
holding our sympathy, our interest, and our respect.

As she experiences the happenings of her life, Rachel's
voice is constantly engaged in sifting, analyzing, and questioning them. George Bowering has written a fine essay on *A Jest of
God*—and only a poet could have examined Margaret
Laurence's techniques of language as he has done:

What happens happens *in* the writing, not in front of
it. One sees through the eye, not with it. Mrs.
Laurence is not talking *about* life; she is trying to
re-enact the responses to it. ("That Fool Of A Fear,"
        Canadian Literature, 50 (Autumn 1971): 55)

Rachel and Mrs. Cameron live in a cosy and, to Rachel,
claustrophobic flat, decorated to her mother's tastes, with
puce-coloured madonna prints, crocheted doilies, and
flowered china. Underneath them is the undertaking
establishment that used to belong to Niall Cameron but now
belongs to Hector Jonas. The princess-in-the-tower must live
with the vulgar, visible evidence of the embarrassment and the
fear that her father's occupation had always meant to her, the
blue neon sign that flashes "Japonica Funeral Chapel" night
and day. She feels a mixture of resentment and envy towards
her sister Stacey—married, with four children, living in
Vancouver. There had not been enough money after her
father's death for Rachel to finish university. Fourteen years
ago, she had come back to Manawaka to teach and to support
her mother.

At this present crisis-point in her life, she cannot find any
dignity at all, either in what she has done or in what she is
doing. Her principal, Willard Siddley, seems a sadist to her; at
the same time she is sickened because she is so aware of his
physical presence. She envies Jimmy Doherty's mother,
Grace, and beats herself with guilt because of her frustrated
maternalism. The fact that she *is* teaching, that she manages to
get through each day and, worst still, each tormented night and
on to the next, that she does manage to support, pamper, and
even feel some indulgence for her mother—all of these facts
mean nothing to her. But the reader sees them. What Rachel is
actually doing plays its counterpoint, limited in range, but
necessary to the novel's success, to what she thinks are her total
failures.

More than anything else, she fears being thought
eccentric, queer, a fool, by her present pupils or the ones she
used to teach, by any one at all—most of all by herself, though

she constantly beats herself with burning ridicule. She refers to herself as some grotesque being—"that giant She," "a stick of chalk," "some ungainly bird." The isolation from which she suffers so much is, in part at least, self-induced; there have been hands stretched out to her, but through fear, or snobbery, or insecurity, she has pushed them away:

> When I first came back to Manawaka, Lennox Cates used to ask me out, and I went, but when he started asking me out twice a week, I stopped seeing him before it went any further. We didn't have enough in common, I thought, meaning I couldn't visualize myself as the wife of a farmer, a man who'd never even finished High School. He married not long afterwards. I've taught three of his children. All nice-looking kids, fair-haired like Lennox, and all bright. Well. (*A Jest of God*, p. 31)

Her colleague Calla offers friendship too, but Rachel is embarrassed by Calla's differentness, by her uninhibited sloppiness and, most of all, by the fundamentalism of her Pentacostal religion:

> If only Calla wouldn't insist on talking about the Tabernacle in Mother's hearing. Mother thinks the whole thing is weird in the extreme, and as for anyone speaking in a clarion voice about their beliefs—it seems indecent to her, almost in the same class as what she calls foul language. Then I get embarrassed for Calla, and ashamed of being embarrassed, and would give anything to shut her up or else to stop minding. (*A Jest of God*, p. 26)

When Rachel does go with Calla to the "Tabernacle of the Risen and Reborn," to her absolute self-degradation she is seized with hysteria and begins to moan and babble as if speaking with tongues. Back at Calla's apartment, she suffers more shock and revulsion when Calla's affection is revealed as a lover's, not a friend's. From that she flies; anger gives her, for once, a self-justification and the power to act.

In the dreary summer holidays Rachel meets Nick Kazlik, a former schoolmate who now teaches in Winnipeg, "the city," and who has come back to his father's farm outside Manawaka for the summer. Her physical need for love outweighs all her crowding doubts and fears: when Nick asks her out she goes; when he kisses her she responds; when he makes love to her she is ready, strong enough in her own desire to trample down all the crowding fears, though miserably shamed by the awkwardness of her virginity. Their love affair runs its course throughout the summer. Rachel schemes to deceive her mother and discovers that she can be ruthless in opposition to her when the issue is something she wants and needs as badly as her hours with Nick. Finally in a burst of self-confidence that follows her first experience of physical release in love, she voices her need for a child—his child:

> If one speaks from faith, not logic, how does that turn out? I do not know, except that I am so strong in it, so assured, that it cannot possibly go wrong.
>
> "Nick—"
>
> "Mm?"
>
> "If I had a child, I would like it to be yours."
>
> This seems so unforced that I feel he must see it the way I do. And so restrained, as well, when I might have torn at him—*Give me my children.*
>
> His flesh, his skin, his bones, his blood—all are still connected with mine, but now suddenly not. Not a muscular withdrawal. Something different, something unsuspected.
>
> His face turns away from mine. He puts his mouth momentarily on my shoulder. Then, still not looking at me, he brushes a hand across my forehead.
>
> "Darling," he says, "I'm not God. I can't solve anything."   (*A Jest of God,* p. 148)

Rachel does not hear from Nick again. As summer ends

and school begins again, she has that loss to bear and the terrible fear and just as terrible hope of pregnancy besides. The present, the past, the questionings, and the fantasies of Rachel are all woven together and their strands join in the aftermath of her affair with Nick Kazlik. As Hagar was, on one level, biblically symbolic, the proud and usurping handmaiden of Abraham and the mother of Ishmael, so Rachel is also symbolically biblical in her "mourning for her children," the children she has never had. Nick is real to Rachel as a lover, and yet she needs him more urgently as a father for her children than as a lover. She cannot understand the depth of his own problem as the son of a Ukranian immigrant and as the child who cannot do for his parents what Steve, his dead brother, would have done. Steve would have preserved the land that Nestor Kazlik loved and would have given himself to it; Nick cannot. He understands Rachel better than she understands him. When he says, "I'm not God, I cannot solve anything," we know the depth of his meaning, but Rachel still has to learn it, painfully. She does not lose Nick, because she never had him in any committed sense, and she does not bear his child as she hoped and feared she would do.

Rachel's real salvation and significance is that she is not a tragic figure, not the character in a drama that she sometimes makes of herself, but just an ordinary human being. In her despair at her possible pregnancy, when the time comes to make the final grand gesture, to take the whiskey and the sleeping pills and throw it all away, she does not and cannot defy and reject life. She adapts to its blows and its demands:

> At that moment, when I stopped, my mind wasn't empty or paralyzed. I had one clear and simple thought.
> *They will all go on in some how, all of them, but I will be dead as stone and it will be too late then to change my mind.*   (*A Jest of God*, p. 170)

And at that point in her ordeal, she makes a concession that is

comparable to Hagar's concession of error, as she finds herself
on her knees:

> I am not praying—if that is what I am doing—out of
> belief. Only out of need. Not faith, or belief, or the
> feeling of deserving anything. None of that seems to
> be so.
>   *Help me.*
>   Help—if You will—me. Whoever that may be.
> And whoever You are, or where. I am not clever. I am
> not as clever as I hiddenly thought I was. And I am
> not as stupid as I dreaded I might be. Were my
> apologies all a kind of monstrous self-pity? How
> many sores did I refuse to let heal?
>   (*A Jest of God*, p. 171)

Rachel has a final humiliation to undergo: her desperate
struggle between acceptance and rejection of the child-to-be is
all brought to anti-climax. The growth within her is not life, but
a kind of random nothingness, a benign tumour:

> All that. And this at the end of it. I was always afraid
> that I might become a fool. Yet I could almost smile
> with some grotesque lightheadedness at that fool of a
> fear, that poor fear of fools, now that I really am one.
>   (*A Jest of God*, p. 181)

Through the torture of her struggle, however, and the reality
of her operation, Rachel does learn to accept and to live with
her limitations and life's. "I am the mother now," the words
she murmured under anaesthetic, become real to her. They
are her key to a degree of freedom and an acceptance of herself
as she is, no tragic heroine, but an ordinary foolish mortal. She
can finally face herself with an equivalent to Prufrock's rueful
"No! I am not Prince Hamlet nor was meant to be." As Nick
could not be God for her, so she cannot and must not be God
for her mother. Her choices are human and humanly limited,
but she does have choices and she makes one of them—the
decision to move. She is no longer afraid to leave Manawaka,

for she is no longer dependent on her fear of the town for a kind of tortured security of identity. She is free of the geographical place, Manawaka, while still knowing and accepting that in the deepest sense the town will be with her forever, both its strengths and its constraints. These she will always carry within her to deal with as she is able. She applies for and is accepted by a school in Vancouver and against all her mother's tears and threats she moves there, taking "her elderly child" with her:

> We watched until the lights of the town could not be seen any longer. Now only the farm kitchens and the stars are out there to signpost the night. The bus flies along, smooth and confident as a great owl through the darkness, and all the passengers are quiet, some of them sleeping. Beside me sleeps my elderly child.
>
> Where I'm going, anything may happen. Nothing may happen. Maybe I will marry a middle-aged widower, or a longshoreman, or a cattle-hoof-trimmer, or a barrister or a thief. And have my children in time. Or maybe not. Most of the chances are against it. But not, I think, quite all. What will happen? What will happen. It may be that my children will always be temporary, never to be held. But so are everyone's.   (*A Jest of God*, p. 201)

The finding of decision and spirit, the affirming of the future, is in Rachel's context a great victory. And the moment of recognition that "I am the mother now" is more than Rachel's, it is everyone's, and it is one of the saddest and strangest moments that life holds. Margaret Laurence has prepared us for this moment in Rachel's life throughout the novel, and specifically on two previous occasions when Rachel has mistakenly or confusedly referred to her mother as her child. Moreover, *A Jest of God* makes a great affirmation of life and living, happening in the midst of and in spite of terrible muddle, anxiety, and confusion. Rachel does not grandly go mad or tragically die like those who would break life to their wills: she bends to life's blows, as most mortals have done before her, and life plays its amazing, everlasting trick once again for her, bringing vitality and at least some hope out of defeat.

Thematically *A Jest of God* is important and convincing in its dignity. In *The Stone Angel*, a Christian pattern is discernible, enclosing Hagar's story and culminating in the symbolic water—the gift of grace. But the resolution of Rachel's story comes existentially, out of her life's present confusion. Here, Margaret Laurence does not call upon any supportive, doctrinal pattern; she works only with and through what meaning might reasonably be expected to come from Rachel's own muddle. On its own terms the book is, however, yet another variation of a religious quest. Repeatedly Rachel says "if I believed," and her moment of release is a prayer to a God whose existence is completely in doubt:

> If You have spoken, I am not aware of having heard.
> If You have a voice, it is not comprehensible to me.
> No omens. No burning bush, no pillar of sand by day
> or pillar of flame by night.   (*A Jest of God*, p. 171)

That cry from her wilderness is no less a cry of Rachel's blind struggle for faith, just because she does not know the direction in which to send it and does not dare to dream or dare to hope that her cry will be heard.*

Her solitary quest for meaning, reassurance, faith, God, has been contrasted and counterpointed throughout the novel, first by the seemingly empty formality of her mother's brand of Presbyterianism and then by Calla's Pentecostal enthusiasm. In her mother's church the figure of Christ at the front is like a "languid insurance salesman." In Calla's Tabernacle the two pictures of Jesus are "bearded and bleeding, his heart exposed and bristling with thorns like a scarlet pincushion." Rachel rejects both ways of worship, but she is herself a child of the

---

*For a study of Rachel's isolation, see C. M. McLay, "Every Man is an Island; Isolation in *A Jest of God*," *Canadian Literature*, 50 (Autumn 1971): pp. 57-68.

Presbyterians and she is particularly ashamed and revolted by Calla's uninhibited worship. She is appalled and sickened by disgrace when she herself is seized with hysterical utterance:

> *That voice!*
> Chattering, crying, ululating, the forbidden transformed cryptically to nonsense, dragged from the crypt, stolen and shouted, the shuddering of it, the fear, the breaking, the release, the grieving—
> Not Calla's voice. Mine. Oh my God. Mine. The voice of Rachel.   (*A Jest of God*, p. 36)

Much later in the book Calla herself is finally granted the gift of tongues and she tells Rachel that to her, "It was peace. Like some very gentle falling of rain." Calla is the friend to whom Rachel goes for help and Rachel is finally humbled by her generosity:

> Maybe she'll pray for me, and maybe, even, I could do with that. But she hasn't said so, and she won't, and that is an act of great tact and restraint on her part.   (*A Jest of God*, p. 176)

In *The Stone Angel*, the Old Testament figure of Hagar in the wilderness is brought forward to the New Testament; the resolution of her story is offered us in New Testament terms. In *A Jest of God*, the Old Testament figure of Rachel mourning for her children is left finally and resolutely in the Old Testament's framework, to show forth whatever meaning is possible in its terms alone. Rachel moves, like her biblical ancestress, through monstrous darkness. Hagar is at first a Grotesque, but she has savoured life; in fact she has been greedy for all its experiences and sensations. Rachel sees both herself and life as Grotesques; she is afraid of her own instincts, and all the life that she can see is distorted, chaotic, terrifying, an enormity of injustice. But finally there *is* a flash of light in her darkness, not much light, but enough to show her where the path lies ahead. Rachel sees that she has "expected justice, without being able to give it." She was looking for an Old Testament's patriarch god, a father-figure who would direct and protect her, and she was also looking for a New Testament's Christ who would redeem her and, quite literally, make her new. She moves finally to a recognition that she must and she will rely on whatever strength she can find or forge within herself:

> I will walk by myself on the shore of the sea and look at the freegulls flying. I will grow too orderly, plumping up the chesterfield cushions just-so before I go to bed. I will rage in my insomnia like a prophetess. I will take care to remember a vitamin pill each morning with my breakfast. I will be afraid. Sometimes I will feel light-hearted, sometimes light-headed. I may sing aloud, even in the dark. I will ask myself if I am going mad, but if I do, I won't know it.
>
> God's mercy on reluctant jesters. God's grace on fools. God's pity on God. (*A Jest of God*, p. 202)

"God's pity on God"—for only God is entirely alone. This is the final, almost light-hearted up-beat of the novel. For even Rachel has her "elderly child" with her and she has ranged herself with the life-affirming among the community of mankind.

A Jest of God's authenticity of person, place, and detail suggests the psychiatrist's casebook. Because everything comes through Rachel's consciousness and because her mind is so completely, believably, neurotically obsessed, she cannot really see the world around her or the people in it, particularly her mother and Nick, the ones who are closest to her. Much of the time these two are almost stereotypes of the selfish mother and casual seducer and, of course, this is essentially how Rachel sees them as she hugs her feelings of inadequacy and injury. From Nick she gets many clues about the complexity of his own problems, his responses to his father and mother, his Ukrainian background, and his need to be himself, not his father's confused image of his dead twin, Steve. But no more than a superficial understanding of Nick can penetrate Rachel's self-absorption and her doomed feeling that their relationship could not possibly become permanent. Finally, we do not understand Nick either. The snapshot he showed her, which she thought was of his son but was really of himself, remains as much a mystery to us as to Rachel.

The characters who are more detached from the centre of Rachel's concern come through with vivid energy and clarity. Sloppy, slap-dash Calla and Hector, the undertaker who took over Niall Cameron's business, take on their own reality, life, and energy. The two scenes, of Calla and Rachel in the Tabernacle, and Rachel and Hector in the undertaking establishment in the dead of night, are the most vividly written in the book, making their impact in the way that is unmistakably one of Margaret Laurence's strongest fortes: the ordinary, commonplace event heightened to the absurd, the grotesque, the hilariously funny, and obscurely terrifying. The effects of each of these incidents on Rachel is a compelling reminder that what is sustaining for one mind is unendurable to another, for the borderline of reality is a shadowy line and beyond it is nightmare as often as dream. In the Tabernacle the climax comes as horror to Rachel and peace to Calla:

> Singing. We have to stand, and I must try to make myself narrower so I won't brush against anyone. A piano crashes the tune. Guitars and one trombone are in support. The voices are weak at first, wavering like a radio not quite adjusted, and I'm shaking with the effort not to giggle, although God knows it's not amusing me. The voices strengthen, grow muscular, until the room is swollen with the sound of a hymn macabre as the messengers of the apocalypse, the gaunt horsemen, the cloaked skeletons I dreamed of once when I was quite young, and wakened, and she said "Don't be foolish—don't be foolish, Rachel—there's nothing there." The hymn-sound is too loud—it washes into my head, sea waves of it.

> *Day of wrath! O day of mourning!*
> *See fulfilled the prophet's warning!*
> *Heaven and earth in ashes burning!*
>   (*A Jest of God*, p. 32)

In the funeral chapel with Hector, what is simple pleasure and pride in his business for him, is hysterical rejection and searing revelation for Rachel;

> The blue light, and the chapel purged of all spirit, all spirits except the rye, and the sombre flashiness, and the terribly moving corniness of that hymn, and the hour, and the strangeness, and the plump well-meaning arm across my shoulders, and the changes in every place that go on without our knowing, and the fact that there is nothing here for me except what is here now—   (*A Jest of God*, p. 127)

Rachel's voice, in the present tense, almost hysterical and yet propelling the reader compulsively onward, is the remarkable achievement of *A Jest of God*. The voice is as taut as an elastic stretched to snapping point, but within its narrow range there is still great variation and density of effect. Hagar's world was filled with colour, movement, and sensual experiences of all kinds; though Rachel thinks of herself as dry and empty, her world is not. It is as teeming with objects and sensations as Hagar's and therefore compelling to the reader. In particular, Rachel's words are laced together by a lavish use of nature-imagery in similes and metaphors which add their extra and sensual dimensions to the text. Bird imagery is especially constant: Rachel sees herself "rising gawkily, like a tame goose trying to fly," or "an ostrich walking with extreme care through some formal garden"; she describes Calla, "looking like a wind-dishevelled owl, a great horned owl, her fringed hair like grey-brown feathers every which way." There are scores of others—"sour as a crabapple," "thin as a thighbone," "like a stick of chalk," "crane of a body, gaunt metal or gaunt bird," "like a dried autumn flower stalk," "an empty eggshell skull." Most of these images refer to Rachel herself, combining the pathetic and the absurd in their effects, but all of them extend the range of Rachel's voice and increase the variety of its effects.

Margaret Laurence recalls trying to write this novel in the third person:

> Everything about those first drafts of the first pages was wrong. They were too stilted; the character of Rachel would not reveal herself. So finally I gave up and stopped struggling. I began to write the novel as I must have very intensely wanted to write it—in the first person, through Rachel's eyes. I knew that this meant the focus of the book was narrow—but so was Rachel's life. I knew I had to be very careful, for Rachel is a potential hysteric who does not for quite a while realize this about herself, but the prose must not be hysterical or it would lose its ability to convey her. I knew that the other characters, viewed only by Rachel, might not emerge as clearly as I wanted them to.
>
> ("Gadgetry or Growing? . . Form and Voice in the Novel")

In the process of writing a novel, Margaret Laurence's identification with her characters is so close that to her they are real persons, feeling, acting—and *speaking*. This empathy, which is a kind of possession of author by characters, is, of course, the source of Rachel's energy, her convincing life. "Rachel," Margaret Laurence says, "was self-perceptive, indeed, a compulsive pulsetaker":

> She saw things about herself which Hagar did not see about *herself*, although Rachel tended to exaggerate vastly her own inadequacies and shortcomings. I hoped that this exaggeration would be plain, not only through Rachel's own obviously loaded assessments of herself, but through Nick's reaction to her. To

Nick, Rachel does not at first seem anything except a
fairly attractive and intelligent woman, and it is only
when Rachel reveals her deep uncertainties to him
that he perceives how desperate is her need and how
little he can fulfil it. No one could fulfil it—she needs
too much. . . .

The present tense of the novel naturally
presented problems in terms of the narrative con-
tinuation—getting from point A to point B, as it
were, and I think there are places in the novel where
this becomes a serious flaw. On the other hand, I felt
that the present tense was essential in order to convey a sense of immediacy, of everything happening
right that moment, and I felt that this sense of immediacy was necessary in order to get across the
quality of Rachel's pain and her determined efforts to
survive.

("Gadgetry or Growing? . . Form and Voice in the
Novel")

A Jest of God moves Manawaka generations forward in
time from Jason Currie and his like, the tough and "God-
fearing" Scots. Rachel is a descendant of the Scots and Nick
Kazlik of Ukrainians who came into the area a little later:

Half the town is Scots descent and the other half is
Ukrainian. Oil, as they say, and water. Both came for
the same reasons, because they had nothing where
they were before. That was a long way away and a
long time ago. The Ukrainians knew how to be the
better grain farmers, but the Scots knew how to be
almightier than anyone but God.

(*A Jest of God,* p. 65)

The strengths that were built into Manawaka by its
pioneers—and also the terrible, inhibiting power of the town's
constraints—are at battle in the person of Rachel Cameron. *A
Jest of God* is the story of Rachel's ordeal and of her limited
victory. She begins totally in chains, some of her own making,

but others of her parents', her ancestors', and the town of Manawaka's. She resents the chains, but at the same time without them she has no identity at all—she could not stand on her own strength. When the book ends she has shaken free the binding-supporting chains, and she realizes the pitiful smallness of her strength. But she also realizes that what strength she has she must use and that Manawaka, an inheritance and the source of her identity, must—and will—go with her always.

SIX

*A Bird in the House;
Jason's Quest*

The creative writer perceives his world once and
for all in childhood and adolescence, and his
whole career is an effort to illustrate his private
world in terms of the great public world we all
share.

Graham Greene, *Collected Essays.*

Seven of the eight stories of Vanessa MacLeod were written in
England from 1962 onwards, and published in various
periodicals in Canada and America and in Macmillan's
Winter's Tales in England. With the addition of "Jericho's
Brick Battlement," they were gathered together as *A Bird in
the House* and published in 1970. Concurrently with the revi-
sion and publication of *The Stone Angel* and with the writing of
A Jest of God, facets of other lives in Manawaka were being
given form, moving from Margaret Laurence's memories and
perceptions into their fictional structures.

Margaret Laurence calls these stories "fictionalized autobiography": her own growth from a child's awareness of the
small, tight world of family to an adolescent's understanding of
the widening circles of the world around her is paralleled by
Vanessa MacLeod's. The deaths of her own parents, the
changes made first by loss and grief and then, inevitably and

relentlessly, by the practical circumstances of her life, are present in Vanessa's story, certainly not in exactitude of detail, but certainly in truth of spirit.

Basic to this work and linking it to the genre of autobiography is the continuum of time as an integral part of its structure. The stories move through ten years of Vanessa's life from about 1935 onward. As she grows, she is aware of the landmarks which have had their continued bearing on her own life and on Manawaka: the emigration of the pioneers to Manitoba, the First and Second World Wars, and climactically the tragedy of Dieppe where so many Manawakan boys, recruits to the Cameron Highlanders, were killed. But only as the adult Vanessa, looking back at her child-self, can she begin to understand her history and all history as "the past," with all its powers over the present in both its challenges and chains.

Most constant, as Vanessa comes to awareness, is the force of the Depression, which impinges on all the stabilities of her life. The Depression forced her Aunt Edna back from Winnipeg to keep house for Grandmother and Grandfather Connor; her father cannot collect bills or hire a nurse or a girl to help with the housework because of the Depression; she and her parents have moved in with Grandmother MacLeod "when the Depression got bad," and the Depression ruined her cousin Chris' bright dreams of education and success:

> The Depression did not get better, as everyone had been saying it would. It got worse, and so did the drought. That part of the prairies where we lived was never dustbowl country. The farms around Manawaka never had a total crop failure, and afterwards, when the drought was over, people used to remark on this fact proudly, as though it had been due to some virtue or special status, like the Children of Israel being afflicted by Jehovah but never in any real danger of annihilation. But although Manawaka never knew the worst, what it knew was bad enough. Or so I learned later. At the time I saw none of it. For me, the Depression and drought were external and

abstract, malevolent gods whose names I secretly learned although they were concealed from me, and whose evil I sensed only superstitiously, knowing they threatened us but not how or why. What I really saw was only what went on in our family.

(*A Bird in the House*, p. 136)

Mysteries surround Vanessa, not only the fears and puzzles of all the things she does not understand in the present, but also the mysteries inexplicably hanging-over from the past. The immediate past of the First World War impinges on her family, a looming factor in her father's decison to become a doctor, in his helpless regret over the death of his brother Roderick and his half-resentful, half-guilty sub-servience to his mother on that account. Vanessa feels these stifling shadows around her in Grandmother MacLeod's house where the touchstone-words are always "I'm sorry." Oppressive though the mysteries are, she finds that a more specific knowledge makes the past unbearable:

He had had to watch his own brother die, not in the antiseptic calm of some hospital, but out in the open, the stretches of mud I had seen in his snapshots. He would not have known what to do. He would just have had to stand there and look at it, whatever that might mean. I looked at my father with a kind of horrified awe, and then I began to cry.

(*A Bird in the House*, p. 93)

Perhaps the prime motivation of these stories was Margaret Laurence's need to exorcise the powerful demons of her own past, particularly the figure of Grandfather Simpson who had inspired in her so much resentment:

I came to write about my own background out of a desire—a personal desire—to come to terms with what I call my ancestral past.

My family began in Scotland and I was brought up with a great knowledge of my Scots background, but it took me a long time—in fact I was really grown up—before I recognized that, in point of fact, these ancestors were very far away from me and that Scotland to me was just an ancestral memory, almost in a Jungian sense. And that, if I came from anywhere, I came from a small prairie town of Scots Presbyterian stock. I had to come to terms in some way with that environment which I had, at the time, rebelled against—I wanted very much to get out—I couldn't wait to get out of that town. Then, years later, I found I had to come back and examine all those things, examine my own family, my own roots and in some way put to rest the threat that had been there. I think that, in a sense, this is what I have done.

("A Conversation About Literature: An Interview with Margaret Laurence and Irving Layton," *Journal of Canadian Fiction* 1, no. 1 (Winter 1972): 66)

In "To Set Our House in Order," Grandmother MacLeod is obsessed by the past and, at her family's cost, tries to live in terms of a past that no longer exists.

"When I married your Grandfather MacLeod," she related, "he said to me, 'Eleanor, don't think because we're going to the prairies that I expect you to live roughly. You're used to a proper house, and you shall have one.' He was as good as his word. Before we'd been in Manawaka three years, he'd had this place built. He earned a good deal of money in his time, your grandfather. He soon had more patients than either of the other doctors. We ordered our dinner service and all our silver from Birks' in Toronto. We had resident help in those days, of course, and never had less than twelve guests for dinner parties. When I had a tea, it would always be twenty or thirty. Never

any less than half a dozen different kinds of cake were
ever served in this house."

(*A Bird in the House*, p. 45)

Grandmother MacLeod also romanticizes the remote
ancestral past, again to the considerable damage of those who
are living in the present:

"All right," my father said tiredly. "We'll call him
Roderick."

Then, alarmingly, he threw back his head and
laughed.

"Roderick Dhu!" he cried. "That's what you'll
call him, isn't it? Black Roderick. Like before. Don't
you remember? As though he were a character out of
Sir Walter Scott, instead of an ordinary kid who—"

(*A Bird in the House*, p. 55)

In "The Sound of the Singing," Vanessa remembers
Grandfather Connor's reminiscences as one of the hazards of
Sunday dinner at the Brick House: "If he could think of
nothing else to do, he would sit me down on a footstool beside
his chair and make me listen, fidgeting with boredom, while he
talked of the past" (*A Bird in the House*, p. 9).

Grandfather Connor is, in fact, the hero of *A Bird in the
House*. He is a fictionalized characterization of Margaret
Laurence's Grandfather Simpson. Grandfather Connor had
been a pioneer in western Canada; he cowed his children and
infuriated his granddaughter Vanessa; but in his own in-
articulate way, he had loved his wife and had been as pitifully
bewildered by the circumstances that defeated and distorted
him as he had been justifiably proud of his many strengths and
achievements. Although Vanessa detested him, she grew to
pity and finally to understand and respect him. For Margaret
Laurence the writing of these stories was a journey back in
time and memory, to exorcise the intimidating ghost of her
grandfather and to sublimate her youthful bitterness towards

him by the processes of art, until all bitterness burned away and the old man became part of her and Canada's past—Grandfather Connor standing not only for Grandfather Simpson but for all the proud, tough, puritanical pioneers who were Canada's "upright men":

> He was a pioneer. He was a very strong, authoritarian old man—I never remember him as anything but an old man. He seemed to be as old as God right from the moment I first had a memory of him. I don't remember the old man expressing any emotion but anger except once—that was when my grandmother died and, horrifyingly, he broke down and cried. This was like having a mountain crumble. I was absolutely appalled: I wasn't even compassionate toward him; I was simply horrified at the granite figure suddenly dissolving. This was the only time he ever did. He had come from Ontario, Ontario Irish—as they use to say in my family, "famine Irish, but thank God Protestant!" He had come out to Manitoba as a young boy of sixteen or seventeen. He had had to quit school when he was twelve, when his father died, to look after his mother and others who were described by my family as no good—and they *were* no good. It was only many years later that I realized how terribly unfair it was that none of us really loved the old man, although he had been the one to support his brothers for many years.
>
> He had as a boy walked from Winnipeg to Portage la Prairie after coming out to Manitoba by steamer. In the short stories in *A Bird in the House*, I have him as a blacksmith and then a hardware merchant: in real life he was a cabinet-maker who became an undertaker as many cabinet-makers did because they made all the coffins. I recall him as a man impossible to please, and I recall myself rebelling desperately against this hard, harsh sort of personality. Yet many years later, thinking of him

and particularly through writing the stories, I realize that all of us in our family have inherited a great many of his characteristics, both good and bad. We all have rather bad tempers. We all have a good deal of tenacity which I think we did inherit from the old man. Only after I had finished writing these short stories did I begin to realize that, although I had detested the old man at the time, I no longer detested him. I had come to some kind of terms with him, whereby I could realize that even though he had been a very hard man, he had had a very hard life and he had characteristics of strength and of pride that were admirable—and the other side of the coin was his inability to show affection. So that it was the sort of puritanical thing with the two-sided coin.

I do think that what sums it up to me are two lines from a poem by Al Purdy; I recall them very, very clearly because they seem to express everything I feel about my grandfather's generation and the generation of Hagar in *The Stone Angel*, They are from a poem called "Roblin Mills"; they are talking about pioneers and they go like this—

> but they had their being once
> and left a place to stand on

—this is right, because this *is* the place that we are standing on. It took me many years to see that in point of fact what we were doing—not just myself, but almost all Canadian writers—was to try in some way to come to terms with our ancestral past, to deal with these themes of survival, of freedom and growth, and to record our mythology. And I think this is really what we have done. . . . People like my grandfather . . . these are our myths, this is our history. We are, perhaps not consciously, but after a while consciously—this is what we are trying to set down now. ("A Conversation About Literature: An

Interview With Margaret Laurence and Irving
Layton," *Journal of Canadian Fiction*, p. 67)

Like the young Margaret Laurence, Vanessa MacLeod is
already, at age nine, an obsessive writer. Her *Pillars of the
Nation* was in truth an early fictional effort of Margaret
Laurence's—and the origin of Manawaka. But the point of
Vanessa's writing in *A Bird in the House* is not only that it is, so
early, her obvious destiny: it is also, and more importantly, a
way of showing how the child was jostled towards perceptions
and understandings of the people around her—towards really
seeing Aunt Edna, for instance. In "The Mask of the Bear"
Vanessa is writing the story of a barbaric queen, "beautiful and
terrible, and I could imagine her, wearing a long robe of
leopard skin and one or two heavy gold bracelets, pacing an
alabaster courtyard and keening her unrequited love" (*A Bird
in the House*, p. 64). Then Jimmy Lorimer comes to visit Aunt
Edna, and Vanessa hears her wisecracking dismissal of his
proposal without understanding. Later she also hears Aunt
Edna crying in the night:

> There arose in my mind, mysteriously, the picture of
> a barbaric queen, someone who had lived a long time
> ago. I could not reconcile this image with the known
> face, nor could I disconnect it. I thought of my aunt,
> her sturdy laughter, the way she tore into the house-
> work, her hands and feet which she always disparag-
> ingly joked about, believing them to be clumsy. I
> thought of the story in the scribbler at home. I
> wanted to get home quickly, so I could destroy it.
> (*A Bird in the House*, p. 78)

Not only a process of emotional maturing is being shown
throughout these stories, but also Vanessa's growing awareness
of appropriate and inappropriate modes of fiction, of the in-
sufficiencies of the high romantic mode for the actual
presentations of life's losses and agonies.

The adult world seen through the eyes of a child, the

maturing of the child, innocence to experience—this is so populated a branch of literature as to constitute a genre in itself. To attempt to stake out a new claim in the field is both a challenge and a hazard to a writer. Here again the problem of "voice" becomes paramount: how was Margaret Laurence to present Vanessa's world as the child understood it unless she let Vanessa speak the story? How was she to project the understanding of Vanessa's older self on the child's world, to fuse the two understandings, to juxtapose them, or to blend them in harmony? Her solution could be compared to a technique of double exposures: the narrator became Vanessa, the woman, who takes on the voice and the attributes of the child she was and, at the same time, remains her present self, far older and wiser in compassion and understanding. Vanessa, the child, was aware of all the surfaces of events; besides, she felt obscurely, confusedly, and often resentfully, all the swirling emotional undercurrents. But she did see as a child, darkly. Vanessa, the adult, draws from each remembered experience more than the sum of its surface parts. In every story the remembering charts some progress in the young Vanessa's experience—steps towards understanding or, where understanding was impossible, acceptance. Usually the two Vanessas blend perfectly, with acceptance but not sentimental indulgence of the older self for the younger; sometimes they quite obviously separate in tone and in the dimensions of their knowledge and vocabulary:

> I was not astonished that my grandmother thought the bloody death of Jonathan was very nice, for this was her unvarying response, whatever the verse. And in fact, it was not strange, for to her everything in the Bible was as gentle as she herself. The swords were spiritual only, strokes of lightness and dark, *and the wounds poured cochineal.*
> (*A Bird in the House*, p. 7) [Italics mine]

In a few instances the technique is not successful and the child, Vanessa, seems a little too contrived, with a cuteness of language as embarrassing as a bad pun: "My grandmother was a Mitigated Baptist. I knew this because I heard my father say, "at least she's not an unmitigated Baptist" (*A Bird in the House,* p. 17). But failures are rare because Margaret Laurence's taste and her restraint in handling her material are remarkably sure.

What finally becomes somewhat oppressive in the collective stories, however (and this would not have been so as they were singly written and published), are the restrictions of their circumference and the sameness of their final effect. Vanessa's world is a small circle, constantly impinged upon or threatened by death, the Depression, fears, and the effects of two world wars. It is a world of harsh edges, muted colours or no colours, in contrast to the irrepressible brilliance of Margaret Laurence's African world in her *The Tomorrow-Tamer* stories. Its surfaces are all rough, and it is dominated by grandfather and the Brick House, symbols of the roughness of all the elements that buffeted Vanessa into maturity. The episodes are convincingly unique to Vanessa, the sensitive but tough-minded child we see growing through these stories; the vivid phrases are true, both to Margaret Laurence's talent and the place, time, and idioms of her people. Yet, there is a fated sameness about Vanessa's path. Each story ends with some recognition that is a step towards maturity; sometimes we finish with a limited child's point of view, as in "To Set Our House in Order":

> I could not really comprehend these things, but I sensed their strangeness, their disarray. I felt that whatever God might love in this world, it was certainly not order.　　　　　　　(*A Bird in the House*, p. 59)

And sometimes the adult Vanessa's perceptions finally beam through to lighten the gloom of Grandfather Connor in her background:

> Many years later, when Manawaka was far away from me, in miles and in time, I saw one day in a museum

the Bear Mask of the Haida Indians. It was a weird
mask. The features were ugly and yet powerful. The
mouth was turned down in an expression of sullen
rage. The eyes were empty caverns, revealing
nothing. Yet as I looked, they seemed to draw my
own eyes towards them, until I imagined I could see
somewhere within that darkness a look which I knew,
a lurking bewilderment. I remembered then that in
the days before it became a museum piece, the mask
had concealed a man.   (*A Bird in the House,* p. 87)

There are, however, two very large bonuses derived from
the collection of these stories into book form. First, *A Bird in
the House* is an integral and necessary part of the pattern of the
Manawaka works as they have evolved. The descriptions of
ordinary people and ordinary things, streets, stores, houses,
rooms in houses, and the everyday life of people in them,
evoke for us the quality of life in Manawaka. Second, in collection they also make a unique contribution to our literature in
a particular Canadian time and place, under the deadening
blows of the Depression and drought of the thirties, and into
the early years of the Second World War. The voice of Aunt
Edna with its carry-over of the "I'll tell the cock-eyed world"
slang of the 1920's is the voice of a Canadian generation whose
chances were killed or, at the very least, constrained for a
decade. And the voices of Vanessa and her first boyfriend,
Michael, as they finish their teens and are thrust, confused,
into the world of the war years, are also the voices of a
generation—Margaret Laurence's and my own.

By his attitudes, Grandfather Connor estranged himself
from his children and his grandchild, but his concept of a
rigid, authoritarian, patriarchal society was as valid to his
generation's vision as it was alien to theirs. And there is,
throughout the course of these stories, a cumulative accretion
to the character of grandfather; he moves away from Vanessa's
childish conception of him as an overbearing, domineering old

man to take on a mythic proportion. Finally, in "Jericho's Brick Battlements," the last story, Margaret Laurence intends—and achieves—a real catharsis of pity for the man and admiration for his type:

> What funeral could my grandfather have been given except the one he got? The sombre hymns were sung, and he was sent to his Maker by the United Church minister, who spoke, as expected, of the fact that Timothy Connor had been one of Manawaka's pioneers. . . .
> He looked exactly the same as he had in life. The same handsome eagle-like features. His eyes were closed. It was only when I noticed the closed eyes that I knew that the blue ice of his stare would never blaze again. I was not sorry that he was dead. I was only surprised. Perhaps I had really imagined that he was immortal. Perhaps he even was immortal, in ways which it would take me half a lifetime to comprehend. . . .
> "You know something, Beth?" Aunt Edna went on, "I can't believe he's dead. It just doesn't seem possible."
> "I know what you mean," my mother said. "Edna—were we always unfair to him?"
> My aunt swallowed a mouthful of rye and ginger ale.
> "Yes, we were," she said. "And he was to us, as well."   (*A Bird in the House*, pp. 204)

Aunt Edna's ironic voice implicates us all. Here, finally, as in some of the African short stories, notably "Godman's Master," Margaret Laurence has fanned out beyond Vanessa's story. She encloses us all in recognition of the inevitability of estrangement and the possibility of understanding between generations and among all men and women.

The story of Jason, the mole, who goes searching for a cure for the invisible sickness that is destroying Molanium and the Molefolk, was published in 1970, the same year as *A Bird in the House*. Unlike Vanessa MacLeod's stories, which were written sporadically from 1962 onwards, Margaret Laurence calls Jason's story "a gift," given her in the summer of 1967 when she was in a period of difficulty with the writing of *The Fire-Dwellers*. Its first draft was completed very quickly. To write a children's book had not been a conscious part of her intention. And indeed, the story as it turns out is validly described on its jacket-flap as for "all ages."

It is the adventure story of Jason, a young mole who ventures through the Great North Tunnel to the world of "Thither" and there meets Oliver, the tawny owl, who like himself is considering going on a quest. Oliver is searching for wisdom which, as an owl, is expected of him, but which he is all too sure he does not have. Oliver and Jason invite two cats, Calico and Topaz, to join them. Calico has been overheard to wish that she could do a noble deed, to prove that cats are fine upstanding creatures; Topaz is along for fun and adventure. They set out together for the city Jason knows as Londinium, carrying with them the magic "Cap of Deeper Thinking" given Jason by the wise leader of the Molefolk, Venerable Mole, with his blessing. They also have the gifts of Jason's mother, Calpurnia, and his sisters, Grace, Beauty, and Faith, and they have the three silver penny pieces that Calico has prudently saved. They meet many adventures, bad and good. They are swindled out of their money by Winstanley the con-cat. It is restored to them by Police Cat Wattles, who modernizes their thinking about Londinium somewhat, and puts them in the way of a lift to Covent Garden on a vegetable lorry.

In London they are threatened and intimidated by the black leather-booted "Blades," who terrorize all the Smaller Animals: they are saved from being run over by a subway train by Mrs. Weepworthy, the former Glitter La Fay of the "Mouse and Mole Troupers." Oliver is captured and put in a cage in the show window of Nicolette's Boutique, but he is rescued by Jason who finds that under stress he can be more daring than he ever dreamed of being. They are all befriended by Madame

Amina of the "Persian Room Cat Boutique," and by Mike, the
night-watch cat. On the Portobello road they find Digger
O'Bucket and his theatrical costumery, "The Mole-Hole."
They give him news of Mrs. Weepworthy—her former self,
Glitter La Fay, was Digger's heart's delight—and so they see
him off to a happy reunion. In turn he gives them a magic
umbrella which helps them to vanquish the Blades in a perilous
confrontation in Marleybone Station. They are befriended by
various Small Animal citizens of London: Joey Blue, the
pigeon, Strine, the Australian cat, and Spice, the Jamaican
one. Oliver is given excellent advice on the gaining of wisdom
by the scholar-owl, Professor Kingsberry; Jason falls in love
with Perdita, the star singer of the Petunia Patch night-club;
and finally, the Blades are entirely vanquished; the Great Rat,
their leader, is killed by his own thugs, and the friends come
safely home again.

In the course of their quest they have found the answers
they were seeking. Oliver's answer lay in Professor Kingsberry's words:

> But I'm afraid I can't tell you how to be wise, Oliver.
> That you must learn for yourself. . . . Knowledge can
> be learned from books. But wisdom, now—wisdom
> must be learned from life itself. I've picked up a
> little, along the way, perhaps, and I fancy that you
> have too, young as you are. You must just go on by
> yourself, and if you have an opinion which turns out
> to be mistaken, Oliver, don't be afraid to change your
> mind, will you? Be patient. When you get home, you
> may be surprised at what you've learned.
>
> (*Jason's Quest*, p. 155)

For Jason, Perdita has unwittingly provided the answer to
the sickness of Molanium:

> "Doesn't anything ever *change* in Molanium, Jason?"
> she asked. "And didn't you ever find life there a
> little—well—dull? The way you describe it, nothing
> ever seems to happen. All this devotion to the past.

It's all very well, history and all that, but surely new things have to happen, too, don't they? I don't think I'd like to live there. Why I'd die of boredom." . . .

"That's it!" he cried. "You've hit on the answer, Perdita! I think I've half known it all along, but I'd never have seen it if you hadn't pointed it out. Molanium has been dying of BOREDOM!" . . .

Everything had to change and grow. . . . But Molanium had been afraid to change. Jason did not yet have a cure, but he felt he knew at last what had been the cause of the invisible sickness. The molefolk had simply stopped caring about life, because nothing new ever happened any more.

(*Jason's Quest*, p. 167)

But of equal importance is the fact that each of the friends has found that one can, and often does, act much more bravely than one feels and that, as Oliver says, "there's good and bad in all tribes. It's your friends that count."

Jason on his quest is like a mirror-image of Vanessa MacLeod, who sensed all too surely that something was wrong, that an "invisible sickness" was at work on the people she loved. Vanessa was powerless, however, to find or effect its cure. Thus *Jason's Quest*, as a part of the large category of "wish-fulfilment" literature among works for children of all ages, acted as a release and a fantasized wish-fulfilment for Margaret Laurence, too. In this work, she was released from the tragic vision and the world of experience into the comic vision and the world of innocence, where the good will always triumph and there is always another day and another chance:

At the onset of dusk in Moleville, the Drums of The Night were heard, played by young moles trained by Perdita and Jason, and at the beginning of dawn, the Trumpets of The Day sounded their silvery notes, telling the molefolk that the night's work was over. .

(*Jason's Quest*, p. 210)

Released and at play in this book, the strengths of Margaret Laurence's talent are very evident. The story is narrated in the third person, but its plot moves forward in large measure by means of dialogue. The speech is easily and swiftly differentiated: Jason with his slightly old-fashioned, elevated diction; the uncertain hesitancy of Oliver's voice, the commonsense flatness of Calico's, and the superficial flightiness, but basic soundness of Topaz'. Mrs. Weepworthy, who has two voices, one for her matter-of-fact self and one for her slightly lugubrious, sentimental memory-self, Glitter La Fay, and Digger O'Bucket, with the stage-Irish of his speech and the goodness of his heart, are small *tours de force* of quick, vivid, and funny characterization. Those who have relatively small parts—Madame Amina, Mike, Wattles, Spice, Strine, and others, are pegged down in our imaginations by vignette scenes and dialogues which establish their individual voices and make them durably memorable. This, and not physical description, is the prime technique of their characterizing:

> Madame Amina was sorting through a counter full of bells and bangles. She came back with a miniature silver bell on a silver chain and slipped it around Topaz's neck. She then stood back to admire the effect, and held up a large round mirror so Topaz could see herself.
>
> "Ah," Madame Amina cried. "Simply perfect! With your colouring, it blends so beautifully. It's *you*, modom!" . . .
>
> At that moment, the nightwatch cat sauntered in. He had been watching the proceedings from the doorway. He put a friendly paw on Madame Amina's shoulder. "Hello, Sal," he said. "How's tricks?" . . .
>
> "Mikey, as ever was!" she exclaimed in quite a different voice from the one she had used before. "Well, haven't seen you in an age, Mike, Must be months since you last dropped in here. How are you? You're looking well. Hush, though, about the name,

luv. Have you forgotten? It doesn't do, not here."

"It's all right," the nightwatch cat said. "These
two ladies are friends of mine. I showed 'em the way
to your shop, Sal."

"Well, I never," said Madame Amina. "Like to
come into the back room for a cuppa tea, all of you?"

(*Jason's Quest*, p. 103)

In the Manawaka works Margaret Laurence's technique
of establishing place is one of evocation rather than the set-
piece description which she had practised in her African
works. In *Jason's Quest* she returns to description, mapping
Molanium and, in particular, describing the Council Hall with
a sun-shower of delighted, detailed invention:

The Great Council Hall, dim and shadowy, was full of
curious objects and ancient slogans chiseled into the
hard-packed earth walls which resembled dull red
brick and glowed faintly in the grey glimmering light
that filtered in from the air shafts. At the front of the
hall was a raised platform, upon which stood the
throne of the Venerable Mole, dark brown polished
oak, high-backed and elaborately carved with twist-
ing earthworms, with a background of grasses and
leaves. Beside the Venerable Mole's chair stood the
standard of Horatio with its marvellously lifelike
woodcarving sheathed in thin-beaten precious
metal—The Golden Mole of the Seventh. The rest of
the Council Hall was filled with the sedate and ornate
chairs of the elders, each with its own family motto;
*Haste Is Idiocy, Bank Your Fires, Slow—Danger
Ahead*, and so on.

On the front wall hung a large tapestry, an ex-
quisite work in subdued tones of blue and rose,
purchased, as Jason explained, at vast expense from
the moles of Bayeux, France, and depicting the later
life and times of Sir Alain de Molyneux, the
bloodthirsty Norman mole who had laid seige to

Molanium at the time of William the Conqueror. The passing of the years, fortunately, had gentled Sir Alain and his followers, and the tapestry showed them dancing around the beribboned Mole Pole on May Day, while flutists fluted and mole maidens threw camomile flowers.

Oliver and Jason examined the cleverly wrought mottoes and slogans which decorated the other walls. The largest was done in scrolled and bedizened lettering, coloured in gold and crimson.

FESTINA LENTE

"The ancient motto of the molefolk," Jason said. "It means *Hurry Slowly.*"   (*Jason's Quest*, p. 13)

In intention *Jason's Quest* is, of course, a moral fable centring on a simple "Forces of Darkness and Forces of Light" confrontation. However, it also intertwines and plays variations on several other themes that are always close to Margaret Laurence's central concerns throughout her writing: the finding and the unexpected presence of courage, one's rightful attitude to the ancestors, and the perilous effects of their overinfluence, and, finally, the inexorable pressure of life on every individual in every society to grow and change. To refuse to do so is to choose death.

All of these themes are made manifest in the relaxed and playful spirit of *Jason's Quest*, a recreational interval in the course of Margaret Laurence's Manawaka works. Their presence demonstrates, as in all of her works, her deepest and most constant concerns.

SEVEN

The Fire-Dwellers

Clear-sighted with a clarity
rarely encountered in dreams
my Explorer-Self stood a little
distant but somewhat fulfilled; behind
him a long misty quest; unanswered
questions put to sleep needing
no longer to be raised.

Chinua Achebe, "The Explorer"
Beware Soul Brother

Stacey MacAindra is Rachel Cameron's sister. She is thirty-nine years old, the wife of Clifford "Mac" MacAindra, a salesman, and the mother of Jen, Duncan, Ian, and Katie, ages two to fourteen. The MacAindras live in a large, slightly shabby house, "not classy, but not run down, either," on Bluejay Crescent in Vancouver. Stacey immediately flings herself at us as a confused, anxious, self-doubting, contemporary housewife: "It's the confusion that bothers me. Everything happens all at once." Stacey is prey to myriads of threatening horrors, both real and imagined, which press in on her from all sides:

Ladybird, ladybird
Fly away home;
Your house is on fire,
Your children are gone.

114

—Crazy rhyme. Got it on the brain this morning. That's from trying to teach Jen a few human words yesterday. Why anybody would want to teach a child a thing like that, I wouldn't know. Half those nursery rhymes are gruesome, when you come to think of it. . . .

Hung above the bed is a wedding picture, Stacey twenty-three, almost beautiful although not knowing it then, and Mac twenty-seven, hopeful confident lean, Agamemnon king of men or the equivalent, at least to her. Sitting on the bed, Stacey sees mirrored her own self in the present flesh, insufficiently concealed by a short mauve nylon nightgown with the ribbon now gone from the neckline and one shoulder frill yanked off by some kid or other.   (*The Fire-Dwellers*, p. 3)

Stacey is the third of the "ordinary" women whom Margaret Laurence has challenged us to recognize as individual and extraordinary—Hagar, old and ugly; Rachel, neurotic spinster, self-obsessed; now the anxious, donkey-on-a-treadmill stereotype, the housewife-and-mother of our time. As in the case of Rachel and Hagar, we are immediately given the pre-eminently important and intriguing signal—neither Stacey's mind nor her imagination is slovenly or commonplace, though to herself she seems in utter disorder. Her consciousness is invaded at all times, from all sides, by her own demands upon herself, by others' demands upon her and needs of her, and by the appalling, unremitting pressures of our world's immediate communications system. In large measure, she is everyman and everywoman in North American urban society: the media *must* be her message because there is no escape from them, nor any other mode of communication that can offer challenge to them. When Stacey sends sos messages out beyond her world, as she often does in her mind, it is with the rueful sense that even God is a victim, as she is:

At the Day of Judgment, God will say *Stacey*

> *MacAindra, what have you done with your life?* And
> I'll say, *well, let's see, Sir, I think I loved my kids.* And
> He'll say, *Are you certain about that?* And I'll say,
> *God, I'm not certain about anything any more.* So
> He'll say, *To hell with you, then. We're all positive
> thinkers up here.* Then again, maybe He wouldn't.
> Maybe He'd say, *Don't worry, Stacey, I'm not all
> that certain either. Sometimes I wonder if I even
> exist.* And I'd say, *I know what you mean, Lord. I
> have the same trouble with myself.*
>
> (*The Fire-Dwellers*, p. 10)

Stacey is far away from both the constraints and the securities
of Manawaka, though its memories still have the power to
move her:

> Stacey Cameron, nearly nineteen, expert typist, hav-
> ing shaken the dust of Manawaka off herself at last.
> Stacey, five foot three, breasts like apples as it says in
> the Song of Solomon. Stacey in scarlet dressmaker
> suit, fussy lace blouse. Good-bye, beloved family.
> Good-bye to the town undertaker, her father,
> capable only of dressing the dead in between bouts
> with his own special embalming fluid. (Dad? I'm
> sorry. But I had to go.) Good-bye to her long-
> suffering mother. (Now I'm not sure any longer what
> lay behind your whining eyes.) Good-bye to Stacey's
> sister, always so clever. (When I think you're still
> there, I can't bear it.)   (*The Fire-Dwellers*, p. 8)

The city she lives in, the society she lives in, and the
consciousness of the wide world that batters her sensibilities
are all chaotic—"all I know is what I read in the papers"—a
universe that seems on the brink of final conflagration. Walking down city streets she is reassured by the size and the
strength of the buildings, "until she looks again and sees them
charred, open to the impersonal winds, glass and steel broken
like vulnerable live bones, shadows of people frog-splayed on

the stone like in that other city" (*The Fire-Dwellers*, p. 11). At night she dreams of fire and her children: *"Only this one can she take with her, away from the crackling smoke, back to the dream world. She must not look to see which one"* (*The Fire-Dwellers*, p. 29). Stacey is the ladybird whose house is on fire and she must live in the torture of that element.

Until they achieved some self-knowledge, both Hagar and Rachel were grotesque and were shown to us as such. Hagar was both monstrous in her physical self and monstrous in her pride and anger of spirit; Rachel was as insubstantial and bodiless as the weird elongated birdlike creature she seemed to herself. We readily saw in her an image of her tortured, uncertain spirit. Now, in *The Fire-Dwellers*, the situation is reversed. It is not Stacey, but Stacey's milieu that is grotesque. Her environment is an apocalyptic world of sudden senseless death: the child run over at the corner of the street; Buckle Fennick, daring death, playing "chicken" with his diesel truck and finally dying when he confronts the driver whose will stays steady for a fraction of a second longer than his own.

More monstrous even than the random death stalking this urban setting is the isolation of its people. Stacey has been terrified lest the child struck by the car at the corner was one of her own; yet she does not find out until weeks later that the child had been Peter Challoner, a friend of Ian's, and that he had been killed. She had no idea of the desperation that lay behind her neighbour Tess' serene and perfectly groomed facade. And when Tess swallows rye and sleeping-tablets, Stacey is wrenched by a sudden understanding of the uncertainty and pathetic insufficiency of Tess's wise-cracking husband, Jake: "I don't know what the hell she *ever* wanted, to tell you the truth. She was so goddam beautiful it seemed incredible that she would marry me at all" (*The Fire-Dwellers*, p. 272).

After Buckle Fennick's death, Stacey goes to find out what happened to his blind mother:

> Yeh, Salvation Army or some do-good bunch like that. It was real funny, the way it happened. The way

I heard it, they told her about the son and said they
was coming back the next day to fetch her off some-
wheres, one of them homes, like, I guess. Well, she
tries to cut her throat, see? Only she can't find the
butcher knife. When they come in the morning there
she was, still crawling around the floor, feeling
everything, but she still hadn't found it. Ever seen
her? Built like the back of a barn, she was. She
must've looked real cute, crawling around on her
hands and knees, with her great big tits bumping
along on the floor, there. (*The Fire-Dwellers*, p. 262)

This is a terrible world, like a vast canvas by Hieronymus Bosch
whose every corner is filled with devilish manifestations of
aberration, cruelty, and desperation, and the whole lit with
hellish flames. It is often surreal, distorted to the very
boundary of the credible and beyond, as in the picture of
Buckle's mother. It is often absurd with a black absurdity and
cruel with a terrifying random cruelty. Its foundation-image of
destructive fire is set off against the constant presence, both in
setting and imagery, of the other element, water.

The old symbols of order have broken down. Mac's father,
Matthew, once a clergyman, is now a figure of pathos, not of
strength or authority. Stacey mourns her loss of secure belief.
She can no longer force the children into forms of worship
which seem empty and inadequate, though she, herself, sometimes nostalgically and regretfully worships:

> *Ye holy angels bright*
> *Who wait at God's right hand*
> *Or through the realms of light*
> *Fly at your Lord's command,*
> *Assist our song,*
> *Or else the theme too high doth seem*
> *For mortal tongue.*

My God, Stacey, what's happened to you,
warbling hymns all of a sudden?

> Nothing. It just came into my head. Used to sing
> it when I was a kid.
> You should tell Dad that. He'd be pleased to
> think you even remembered. Hey—what's up,
> honey? You're not crying, are you?
> No. Eyelash in my eye.
>
> (*The Fire-Dwellers*, p. 71)

And the new symbols of authority—TV ("the Eye"), radio,
newspaper, films, businesses such as Polyglam plastics or
Richalife Vitamins, which exploit people's fear and vanity—are
terrifying in their power.

Stacey MacAindra is a woman who looks at herself at all
times with unremitting honesty, and who, like her sister
Rachel, sees all of her negatives and few of her positives. She
has a far more stable sense of herself than Rachel, however;
while Rachel is forever likening herself to birds or inanimate
objects, Stacey is acutely, constantly, but also reassuringly
aware of the corporeal self—"I wish I lived in some country
where broad-beamed women were fashionable." And although
everything pushes her own absurdities and inadequacies at
her, she survives, in part, by talking back. Stacey's nature is a
compound of love, commonsense, imagination, and humour.
Though she does not think so, she is very strong. She is also
introspective, constantly sifting and questioning her
perceptions and the experiences she has. But she does not
carry on a constant attack upon herself, rather she engages in a
dialectic with herself. Often her self-doubts are moderated by
her own sense of absurdity, and sometimes by a sheer, tough
refusal to lie down under them. For instance: Stacey is too fat.
She constantly promises herself a banana diet. She is dowdy.
She constantly sees herself as others, she thinks, will see her:

> —What's she seeing? Housewife, mother of four,
> this slightly too short and all too amply rumped
> woman with coat of yesteryear, hemlines all the
> wrong lengths as Katie is always telling me, lipstick
> wrong colour, and crowning comic touch, the hat.

> *Man, how antediluvian can you get?*
> (*The Fire-Dwellers*, p. 12)

Then in her own mind, Stacey answers back and is released by her own absurdity:

> Is that what she's thinking? I don't know. But I still have this sense of some monstrous injustice. I want to explain. *Under this chapeau lurks a mermaid, a whore, a tigress.* She'd call a cop and I'd be put in a mental ward.   (*The Fire-Dwellers*, p. 12)

And on many other occasions she is bolstered and strengthened by her own commonsense defiance of her demons:

> I see the dead faces in a mocking procession, looking at me, looking again, shrugging, saying *There's stability for you.* Do I deserve this? Yes, and yet goddammit, *not* yes.   (*The Fire-Dwellers*, p. 7)

A strong counterpoint to the dialogue that goes on all the time inside of Stacey's head is her dynamism. She is a doer, an activator. She is spurred to action both by the needs of her family and by her own nature. We first saw Rachel behind her schoolroom window, separated from the children in the schoolyard and, symbolically, from active, on-going life itself. We first see Stacey in the act of getting out of bed—"c'mon, fat slob, get up off your ass and get going." Rachel was paralyzed, held by her chains and also supported in her paralysis by them: Stacey's frustrations almost overpower her only when her actions cannot be equal to the demands of the situation, when the act of speaking words, for instance, cannot result in real communication between herself and Mac. Or when, watching her children, she can *do* nothing about Katie's vulnerability at fourteen; Ian's stiff, withdrawn pride; Mac's misunderstandings of Duncan; and Jen's inability—or unwillingness—to talk.

Stacey is both a very strong woman and a very maternal one. At the beginning, Mac is effectively outside her circle of herself and children: "I've aged this guy. I've foisted my kids on him." Her guilt is for saddling Mac with their responsibility, not for tacitly excluding him. She honours him for accepting the family, working, and humbling his pride in the work he must do. In fact she feels, intermittently, a great guilt about that. But only at the end of the book, after Duncan nearly drowns, does Stacey see that she has not really wanted to admit Mac to full and equal parenthood with her:

> —He's never held Duncan before, not ever. Why did I think he didn't care about Duncan? Maybe he didn't, once. But he does now. Why didn't I see how much, before? He never showed it, that's why. . . .
> —That's the most Mac will ever be able to say. They're not like me, either of them. They don't want to say it in full technicolor and intense detail. And that's okay, I guess. Ian gets the message. It's his language, too. I wish it were mine. All I can do is accept that it is a language and that it works, at least sometimes. (*The Fire-Dwellers*, p. 295)

Stacey's terms, until now, have included a belief in and a prescription for verbal communication that she now knows she must relinquish.

Beset by crowding anxieties and the grotesqueries of the world she experiences and perceives, an identity less strong than Stacey's could be disintegrated by the series of shocks she receives in the weeks before her fortieth birthday. Instead, her nature is modified, a little, by them. The gifts of chance or, perhaps, of the God she speaks to as "Sir,"—Duncan's life, Jen's words—are finally accompanied by more acceptance of herself, of Mac, and of the irreversible processes of life. The fires outside remain, however: "She feels the city receding as she slides into sleep. Will it return tomorrow?" (*The Fire-Dwellers*, p. 308).

The simple time-continuum of *The Fire-Dwellers*,

through the few weeks before Stacey's fortieth birthday, gives
a rational, logical basis to the novel. However, its important
movement is an *expansion* from this time-line, not a journey
into acceptance as in *The Stone Angel*, or a step-by-step
journey into the self as in *A Jest of God*. The consciousness of
Stacey Cameron is like an eye: its pupil expands to accept her
world, then contracts in terror; the movement is a halting,
opening and shutting, a broadening and then a narrowing, and
the final point of poise in the novel is not Stacey's coming to a
revelation or to any new point of departure, but her acceptance
of her own kind of sensitivity, her own ways of seeing and
understanding others—and herself:

> I used to think there would be a blinding flash of light
> some day, and then I would be wise and calm and
> would know how to cope with everything and my kids
> would rise up and call me blessed. Now I see that
> whatever I am like, I'm pretty well stuck with it for
> life. Hell of a revelation that turned out to be.

> —Will the fires go on, inside and out? Until the
> moment when they go out for me, the end of the
> world. And then I'll never know what may happen in
> the next episode.   (*The Fire-Dwellers*, pp. 298, 307)

Stacey lives hectically in the midst of a force-field of
emotions and events that ram and batter her from all sides.
Mac takes a job with Richalife Vitamins. Stacey is appalled by
the thinly masked brutality of his boss, Thor Thorlakson, and
equally by the shoddy, pseudo-"gospel" of Richalife. She
drinks too much at a party and to Mac's rage and disgrace, tells
Thor how she feels. Buckle Fennick, Mac's old friend and
war-comrade, whom Stacey dislikes but also finds attractive,
takes her for a ride in his truck; then back at his place, with his
blind old mother sitting in the room drinking port from a
battered teapot, Stacey finds that Buckle only enjoys sex with
himself—but with her as onlooker. When Buckle tells Mac that
he and Stacey have been to bed together and Mac accuses her,

she is outraged and insulted. Her reaction is, however, not despair, but *action*. She gets into the car, drives to the seashore and meets a young artist, Luke Venturi. Twice later she goes back to his isolated cabin and makes love with him.

There is never any question, for Stacey, of abandoning her responsibilities permanently. Luke's function for her is symbolic of the biblical Luke's—he is a physician to her. He identifies her with water and calls her Merwoman, because she was suddenly there, on the seashore in front of his cabin. Stacey welcomes a temporary unreality and she enjoys the play-mystery of her Merwoman role. She also enjoys sex with Luke as if she had been starved for it for a very long time. He sees her quite simply and exclusively as a woman; therefore, he helps her to see herself momentarily as a singular being, freed of the kaleidoscopic wife-mother-housekeeper roles in which others see her and with all of which, simultaneously, she constantly tries to identify herself. Furthermore, Stacey's brief affair with Luke provides her with a real guilt, the guilt of unfaithfulness to Mac. Psychologically, it is possible for her to deal with this and to know that she must live with it, that for her there can be no such luxury as confession to Mac. Her former tortures of vague guilts and desperations were partly intolerable because they had no focus—they were insidiously debilitating.

Then the ocean, which she has loved as a mysterious but free element, betrays her too: when Duncan is almost drowned Stacey has to recognize once and for all that, dangerous and frightening as the fire-element is, neither she nor the ones she loves can move to or live in any other. Her own weeks of intensified flame have, however, had a clarifying effect on her. She can now acknowledge to herself her acceptance of what she cannot change. She begins to recognize that words do not fully translate experience, nor can they be put in its place. She loses the naïve expectation that words alone can signify either satisfying or unselfish communication between human beings. And she also recognizes that headlong action is no answer to any of her problems. Humour Stacey began with: endurance she has developed. But the patience and the wisdom of balance, of changing what she can change, of accepting what she cannot change and, above all, of knowing the difference between the two, she must learn. Indeed, she *wills herself* to learn:

> —Okay, Stacey, simmer down. The fun is over. It's been over for some time, only you didn't see it before. . . . When we've got all·four kids through university or launched somewhere, and Mac retires and is so thin you have to look twice to see him and I'm so portly I can hardly waddle, we can go to Acapulco and do the Mexican hat dance. I can't stand it. I cannot. I can't take it. Yeh, I can, though. By God, I can, if I set my mind to it.
>
> (*The Fire-Dwellers*, p. 289)

The Fire-Dwellers is technically the most complex of the three novels—a fast-shuttering, multiscreen camera and soundtrack technique. Margaret Laurence has described her difficulties in "orchestrating" the whirling, kaleidoscopic facets of Stacey's mind and imagination, never static but desperation-impelled with energy:

> The main need was for some kind of form which would convey the sense of everything happening all at once, simultaneously. Obviously, if you are trying to get across the vast number of things which impinge upon the individual consciousness every minute of the day, you must be very selective and hope to convey quite a lot by implication rather than quantitative description. Either that, or write a novel of fifty thousand pages, which was very far from being my aim. In fact, I wanted to write something in a kind of prose which would be more spare and pare it down than anything I have ever done before. . . . Narration, dreams, memories, inner running commentary—all had to be brief, even fragmented, to convey the jangled quality of Stacey's life.

I did not want to write a novel entirely in the first person, but I did not want to write one entirely in the third person, either. The inner and outer aspects of Stacey's life were so much at variance that it was essential to have her inner commentary in order to point up the frequent contrast between what she was thinking and what she was saying.

Stacey had been in my mind for a number of years. I almost knew too much about her and her family. I was often overcome with the absolute impossibility of getting enough of it into a novel, while at the same time leaving out much of the strictly domestic detail, such as cleaning the house, which in fact occupied much of her time but was not likely to make very thrilling reading. Maybe I did not put enough of this sort of detail in. . . .

In any event, the novel gave me much trouble in the beginning. I had begun it several times, and each time discarded it because the form did not seem to be conveying the characters and the real dilemmas. I even once burned, dramatically, nearly a hundred pages of a second draft, and then sat down at my typewriter and wrote a deeply gloomy letter to a friend, which began "I am a fire bug."

I even thought the novel should be written in three or four columns, newspaper style, with three or four things happening simultaneously. Luckily, it occurred to me in time that few readers were likely to have three or four pairs of eyes.

I had—or felt I had—perhaps rather too many interlocking themes to deal with, but these were all inherent in Stacey and her situation, so no one thread could be abandoned without weakening the total structure, and yet I was appalled at the number of threads . . . to me at the time they seemed multitudinous—the relationship between a man and woman who have been married many years, when the woman does not have any real area of her life which is her own; the frustration of Stacey in trying to communicate with Mac and her ultimate realization of his bravery and his terrible hangups in having to deal with his problems totally alone; the relationship between generations—Stacey and Mac in relation to their children, as parents, and to their own parents as children; the sense of anguish and fear which Stacey feels in bringing up her kids in a world on fire; and also the question of a middle-aged woman having to accept middle age and learn how to cope with the essential fact of life, which is that the process of life is irreversible. So—these themes. But how to express these things in Stacey's dilemma without saying them in so many words, without actually ever stating them?

Finally the form and the material sorted themselves out. I was, I think, considerably influenced, although subconsciously, by years of TV watching. I kept thinking, "What I want to get is the effect of voices and pictures—just voices and pictures." I became obsessed with this notion, as it seemed to convey the quality of the lives I wanted to try to get across. It was only much later that I realized that "voices and pictures" is only another—and to my mind, better—way of saying "audio-visual." Except, of course, that both voices and pictures in a novel have to be conveyed only through the printed word—although in the future this may change, and some day I would dearly love to write a novel which was illustrated in some kind of bizarre way by a really good artist. In any event, I wanted the pictures—that is, the descriptions, whether in outer life or dreams or memories, to be as sharp and instantaneous as possible, and always brief, because it seemed to me that this is the way—or at least one way—life is perceived, in short sharp visual images which leap away from us even as we look at them.

I decided that a certain amount of external

narration was necessary, partly to avoid the awk-wardness of forward-moving which had plagued *A Jest of God,* and partly to give some distance to the reader's view of Stacey, for she was not the shut-in and withdrawn person that Rachel was.

The inner monologue, of course, is strictly in Stacey's voice, and it was through this, largely, that I hoped to convey her basic toughness of character, her ability to laugh at herself, her strong survival instinct.

Her memories were set to one side of the page in an attempt to clarify the fact that these are flashing in and out of her mind while she is doing other things. They are not flashbacks, nor do they occur in any chronological order. They are snatches, fragments from the past, because this seemed to me to be the way my own memories returned, and it appeared to me that the same would be true of Stacey, whose life is busy and, indeed, often frantic.

The dreams and fantasies were put in italics only in order to identify them as dreams and fantasies, and also, perhaps, to provide a kind of visual variety on the page—something I have myself felt a need for, sometimes, in reading novels—that no one poem should go on too long, that there should be some visual break—and I think that our need for this kind of variety has been conditioned by films and TV.

The reason that I did not use any quotation marks in *The Fire-Dwellers* for the characters' speech to one another was that I wanted to get once again the sense of everything happening all at once, the way in which talk flows in and out of people's lives and is not cut off or separate from events. The reason that some sentences in Stacey's and Mac's talk are unfinished or simply trail off is because that is the way they talked and, in fact, the way many people talk. I did not use "he said" or "she said," because I hoped that the tone of voice and what was being said would be enough to identify each speaker, although I

do identify the speaker fairly often before the conversation begins, and also sometimes the characters
happen to call each other by their names. I had to
check this particular identity method very carefully,
however, when I was rewriting the novel, to try to
make sure that it wasn't being used as a method, but
only when they *would* speak each other's names.
("Gadgetry or Growing? . . Form and Voice in the
Novel.")

A growth in the ability to transmit energy to the page can
be seen throughout Margaret Laurence's work. It is quite
possible to see Hagar with some distance between ourselves
and her, and we are meant always to see the distance between
the Hagars, young and old. Rachel is capable of a constant and,
at times, a cruel detachment from herself, and by the same
token, we can remain detached from her. But Stacey is more
taxing and, on her own terms, triumphant, because she
clamours for attention, demanding the immediacy of our total
consciousness and involvement, whether in approval, in dis-
may, or in rueful laughter. Both Hagar and Rachel hold
themselves apart from other men and women, one from pride
and the other from a kind of fear that is really an inversion of
pride. They are self-designated as "different" and "special"
people—only at the end of their stories do they moderate into
willing members of the tribe of man. In contrast, Stacey is
always *in* life, not apart from it, striving to reach others, not to
separate herself from them. She thinks of herself as commonplace and ordinary, but the great achievement of her anxious,
rueful, urgent voice is to reveal her extraordinary qualities of
love, fortitude, and, especially, vitality.

For *The Fire-Dwellers*, as for the first two Manawaka
novels, the voice of the protagonist is at one with and in-
divisible from the form of the novel. Margaret Laurence
finishes her outline of the techniques used in presenting the
voice of Stacey this way:

No form, of course, really ever succeeds as one would like it to; the finished novel is never as good as the one which existed in the mind. But that is a condition of this profession, and one must accept it.

Earlier in her article, Margaret Laurence had commented on her notion of "form" in the novel:

I have never thought of form and means of expression (I refuse to use that odious "style") as having any meaning in themselves. I am not concerned at all about trying forms and means of expression which are new simply for their own sake or for the sake of doing something different. . . . I am concerned mainly, I think, with finding a form which will enable a novel to reveal itself, a form through which the characters can breath. When I try to think of form by itself, I have to put it in visual terms—I see it not like a house or a cathedral or any enclosing edifice, but rather as a forest, through which one can see outward, in which the shapes of trees do not prevent air and sun, and in which the trees themselves are growing structures, something alive.　　　("Gadgetry or Growing? . . Form and Voice in the Novel")

The form of *The Fire-Dwellers* *is* the voice of Stacey, orchestrated around a short, tight time-sequence—nothing like the lifetime-in-flashbacks of Hagar's memory, or the length of a summer in Rachel's life. Technically, the novel is an exercise in the laying bare of an entire consciousness in all the complexities of its ever-changing present. The novel was written in England between 1966 and 1968 and published in 1969. It is a double experiment, both in channelling all of the facets of Stacey's consciousness into one voice, and in achieving its primary, necessary illusion—the *sound* of Stacey's voice in the words on the page.

EIGHT

The Diviners

remember also your children
for they in their time will want
a place for their feet when
they come of age and the dance
of the future is born
for them.

Chinua Achebe, "Beware, Soul Brother,"
Beware Soul Brother.

The Diviners is the story of Morag Gunn of Manawaka, a writer
of novels. On one level the story unfolds the process of Morag's
life from the death of her parents when she was very young, to
today, the novel's present, when she is forty-seven, long since
divorced from Brooke Skelton, her English professor husband,
and caught up in a tormenting concern for the eighteen-year-
old Pique, the daughter of Morag and Jules Tonnerre. At the
same time Morag is coping with the exacting, frustrating, but
inevitable process of her own work, the writing of her fifth
novel. Bound up in the story of Morag's life is the story of a
writer's struggle to be born and to grow, an explicit and diverse
exploration of one woman's experience of the craft of fiction in
our time and in our society. Implicit in Morag's story is also the
explanation and the insistent ratification for the whole
enterprise of fiction—as an essential illumination of individual
experience and a fleshing out of history into wholeness, from

130

the life of an individual to a complex of lives and events and then to an entire culture, its myths, and legends. Gradually, the book shows us that there are many diviners; the writer who selects from the chaotic complexity of events to give certain moments and certain processes meaning and permanence for a person—or a people—is one of these. In its deepest and broadest meaning, *The Diviners* is the story of a profoundly religious pilgrimage, the affirmation of faith and the finding of grace. In this sense, the novel is the culmination of the Manawaka works; not only do ravelled strands from the lives and events of the other books come together here, but *The Diviner*'s final statement encircles, encloses and completes them all and then rays timelessly outward from their circle:

> The inheritors. Was this, finally and at last, what Morag had always sensed she had to learn from the old man? She had known it all along, but not really known. The gift, or portion of grace, or whatever it was, was finally withdrawn, to be given to someone else. (*The Diviners*, p. 369)

Margaret Laurence has said that she would like the five Manawaka works to be read, essentially, as one work. They are all infused with movement, processes of living, adapting, aspiring, achieving, and dying. Their characters are intense and believable men and women. They are recognizable through the energy of their voices, the urgency of their dilemmas, and the sheer dynamic power of their personalities. Now in the description of the river with which *The Diviners* starts and ends, there is both acceptance and affirmation of the flux of time and energy through all the generations of mankind. At the beginning:

> The river flowed both ways. The current moved from north to south, but the wind usually came from the south, rippling the bronze-green water in the opposite direction. This apparently impossible contradiction, made apparent and possible, still

> fascinated Morag, even after the years of river-
> watching.   (*The Diviners*, p. 3)

And as the novel ends:

> The waters flowed from north to south, and the
> current was visible, but now a south wind was blow-
> ing, ruffling the water in the opposite direction, so
> that the river, as so often here, seemed to be flowing
> both ways.
>   *Look ahead into the past, and back into the
> future, until the silence.*   (*The Diviners*, p. 370)

A much longer work than the other Manawaka novels, *The Diviners* is structured in five parts. The first and the fifth, "River of Now and Then" and "The Diviners," are brief chapters of introduction to Morag's present crisis and its resolution about two months later, each approximately fifteen pages long. The three interior sections, "The Nuisance Grounds," "Halls of Sion," and "Rights of Passage," are all close to the same length, about 125 pages. They are of the same basic dramatic structure, rising gradually to a climactic event which marks off one stage and heralds one major change in Morag Gunn's life and growth in sensibility. The five parts form a structure that is epic in both its intention and its techniques; its balance and coordination are an achievement of great complexity. Margaret Laurence's urge has always been towards a tightness of structure that not only contains her words but also grows organically from them. The structure of *The Diviners* is a very real return to, but also an intricate development from, the circular structure of some of *The Tomorrow-Tamer* stories, in particular of "Drummer of All the World." In *The Diviners*, Margaret Laurence is dealing with the longest, most complicated prose-narrative that she has written, with a great increase in the challenges and perplexities of weaving a complex of persons, places, and time together. To answer the technical challenge that this presents, she has devised a structure whose basic pattern formed the skeleton of her first published story.

Hagar compelled our immediate attention by the strong, sardonic tone of her voice and by the reaches of her imagination; Rachel we saw first imprisoned behind her schoolroom window and then we heard the frantic voice imprisoned in her skull; Stacey threw herself at us and clamoured for attention—all of these spoke directly to us in the first person. Morag's tone of voice, immediately struck, is far lower-keyed than these others, and we are relatively distant from her because much of her story is told in the third person. "River of Now and Then" begins with a quiet river image and then introduces Morag as a watcher:

> The dawn mist had lifted, and the morning air was filled with swallows, darting so low over the river that their wings sometimes brushed the water, then spiralling and pirouetting upward again. Morag watched, trying to avoid thought, but this ploy was not successful. (*The Diviners*, p. 3)

These sentences put Morag quietly in her setting, watching, as the next paragraph shows her a watcher, by necessity, on the sidelines of her daughter Pique's life. Only then is this first illusion of distance, of ourselves as watchers of Morag, dispelled, and we are brought right into her presence by her ironic, first-person voice:

> I've got too damn much work in hand to fret over Pique. Lucky me. I've got my work to take my mind off my life. At forty-seven that's not such a terrible state of affairs. If I hadn't been a writer, I might've been a first-rate mess at this point. Don't knock the trade. (*The Diviners*, p. 4)

The narrative voice of *The Diviners*, an element that has been of crucial importance in all the novels, is neither the third person with its implied objectivity, nor the first person with its implied subjectivity, but the abrupt interplay, the constant oscillation between the two, usually signalled throughout the text by a switch from Roman type to italics. Furthermore there is an immediacy about the third-person narrative, which is designed to cancel out any feeling of the author describing Morag from the outside; instead, we are captured by the illusion of Morag describing herself. An early paragraph which ends by giving us necessary information about setting and characters begins with personal fragments of impression:

> The house seemed too quiet. Dank. The kitchen had that sour milk and stale bread smell that Morag remembered from childhood, and which she loathed. There was, however, no sour milk or stale bread here—it must be all in the head, emanating from the emptiness of the place. Until recently the house was full, not only Pique but A-Okay Smith and Maudie and their shifting but ever-large tribe. Morag, for the year when the Smiths lived here, had gone around torn between affection and rage—how could anyone be expected to work in such a madhouse, and here she was feeding them all, more or less, and no goddamn money would be coming in if she didn't get back to the typewriter. Now, of course, she wished some of them were here again.
>
> (*The Diviners*, p. 4)

This illusion is given credence in our minds by Morag's being a writer, a fact we are not only told, we are shown. Morag works with words and she plays with them; she is constantly and obsessively translating experience and impression, from anxiety about Pique to wonder at the swallows, into her medium, the word:

> The swallows dipped and spun over the water, a streaking of blue-black wings and bright breast-

feathers. How could that colour be caught in words?
A sort of rosy peach colour, but that sounded corny
and was also inaccurate.

I used to think that words could do anything.
Magic. Sorcery. Even miracle. But no, only occa-
sionally.   (*The Diviners*, p. 4)

Morag comes to us then as perforce a watcher, first by the
terms of her life, in the present stage of her relationship with
Pique, and also by the terms of her profession. She is far from
calm, but she is becalmed. She is not powerless to act, but at
this point in her life the opportunities for dynamic action do
not exist in her relationships with others. They only exist when
her work is going well, in the act of writing her fiction.

Thinking of Pique, who has gone away leaving only a
"Don't worry" note stuck in the typewriter, wondering
whether or not she will go to visit Manawaka, Morag gets out
her old snapshots and becomes a watcher in a third sense, a
watcher on her own past life. Here Margaret Laurence introduces the first of two major variations on the flashback
narrative technique that form large sections of the fabric of *The
Diviners*. In the text they are always headed Snapshot and
Memorybank Movie. The first is a description of an old
snapshot; the words catch a scene from the past, but it is
perfectly static. The words Morag attaches to the snapshots call
up questions that cannot now be answered. They relate
fantasies she remembers composing: *"I keep the snapshots not
for what they show but for what is hidden in them"* (*The
Diviners*, p. 6). As she looks at the snapshots she is aware that
her particular "reading" of each one of them goes a long time
back. She has forged her past out of the material of her
memories by selecting, interpreting, and fantasizing. As a
writer Morag is particularly aware of herself as an interpreter
of her own memories. The snapshots take her through
fragments of her very early years:

Some people wouldn't have allowed a dog to sleep at

the foot of the bed, but Morag's mother doesn't mind, because she knows Morag wants Snap to be there so she will feel safe. Morag's mother is not the sort of mother who yells at kids. She does not whine either. She is not like Prin.

All this is crazy, of course, and quite untrue. Or maybe true and maybe not. I am remembering myself composing this interpretation, in Christie and Prin's house.   (*The Diviners*, p. 7)

Morag remembers what happened after the taking of a particular snapshot and then: *"I don't recall when I invented that one. I can remember it though, very clearly. Looking at the picture and knowing what was in it. I must have made it up much later on"* (*The Diviners*, p. 8).

The last snapshot, which includes the spruce trees around the house she was born in, "has hidden in it" her imaginary playmates, Blue-Sky Mother, Rosa Picardy, Cowboy Joke, and the rest, and brings her to the time of her mother and father's death:

> *But I remember it, everything. Somewhat ironically, it is the first memory of actual people that I can trust, although I can't trust it completely, either, partly because I recognize anomalies in it, ways of expressing the remembering, ways which aren't those of a five-year-old.*   (*The Diviners*, p. 11)

Unlike the static snapshots, Memorybank Movies are action and dialogue scenes, third-person narrative "stories" of remembered events and past periods in Morag's life. The first one, "Once Upon A Time There Was," covers a brief time-span, the days of the sickness and death from polio of her parents, Colin and Louisa Gunn. As *The Diviners* goes on, the Memorybank Movies sometimes cover long stretches of time with a film's combination of visuality and dialogue. "Once Upon A Time There Was" ends with the farm gates shutting on Morag's childhood and, symbolically, on her Eden: "Morag does not look back, but she hears the metallic clank of the farm gate being shut. Closed." Morag is taken to live in Manawaka with Christie and Prin Logan.

In just over ten pages, "River of Now and Then" has given us the polar points of Morag's experience—her foreground, its river setting, her present combination of personal and professional concerns, and her background, the beginning of her life in the farm outside of Manawaka. She has been established through the variety in her own voice and the major narrative techniques that Margaret Laurence will use throughout the novel. What follows in *The Diviners* is an unfolding of both the time lines, not by precisely measured segments, although both unfold chronologically, but in joining curves as Morag's past feeds into, complicates, explains, and finally is part of the resolution of her present. Her own voice ends "The River of Now and Then," contemplating in herself the flow of generations, Morag's—and *The Diviners'*—deepest concern: *"I remember their deaths, but not their lives. Yet they're inside me, flowing unknown in my blood and moving unrecognized in my skull"* (*The Diviners*, p. 15).

PART II, THE NUISANCE GROUNDS, CHAPTERS TWO, THREE, FOUR

In the three chapters of Part II, "The Nuisance Grounds," Morag's present climaxes in two phone calls, one from Pique's father, Jules Tonnerre, and then a call from Pique herself in Winnipeg. These calls are separated by Morag's witness of her neighbour Royland's successful water-divining on the Smith's property. In the present, little time has elapsed, but in terms of the Memorybank Movies of her past, Morag has moved through all her Manawaka years to the point of leaving for the University of Manitoba at age nineteen. Each of the three chapters begins with Morag's present and makes its transition into the Memorybank Movies naturally and quietly:

The films were beginning again. Sneakily unfolding

inside her head. She could not even be sure of their
veracity, nor guess how many times that they had
been refilmed, a scene deleted here, another added
there. But they were on again, a new season of the old
films.   (*The Diviners*, p. 23)

The films that relentlessly play themselves over and over in her
memory are all of a piece with the other recurrent experiences
of her solitary times—her examination and description of her
mirrored self, the talking to herself Royland teases her about,
and her bemused, ironic, imaginary conversations with
Catharine Parr Traill, an early settler in the same area.

Royland is her neighbour, confidante, counsellor and
friend. Beyond this, his gift of divining water is mysteriously
important to Morag. Royland is a kind of Shaman to her, and
she can see the actual evidence of his power whenever she
watches him divine a well. Through knowing him, Morag
gradually recognizes other "diviners"; he is as low-key a
character in the book as Morag herself, but he and his gift form
the hinge on which the book's deepest meaning turns:

Morag had once tried divining with the willow wand.
Nothing at all had happened. Royland had said she
didn't have the gift. She wasn't surprised. Her area
was elsewhere. He was divining for water. What in
hell was she divining for? You couldn't doubt the
value of water. . . .
    The tip of the willow wand was moving. In
Royland's bony grip, the wood was turning, moving
downwards very slowly, very surely. Towards the
earth.
    Magic, four yards north of the Smith's
clothesline.   (*The Diviners*, p. 83)

In contrast to the quiet, ordinary quality of the
characterizations of Morag and Royland and the low key of
their voices, scenes and characters within the Memorybank
Movies are full of sound, movement, energy, colour, and
drama. The drama of her Manawaka years with the Logans is

introduced by a multisensory, wide-angle lens camera-setting, from *"I can smell the goddam prairie dust on Hill Street, outside Christie's palatial mansion"* through the surroundings of Hill Street, to the valley where "the grass there was high and thick, undulating greenly like wheat," up again to Hill Street, "The Other Side of the Tracks . . . inhabited by those who had not and never would make good," and finally, Christie's house:

> *A square, two-storey wooden box. . . . Front porch floored with splintered unsteady boards. The yard a junk heap, where a few carrots and petunias fought a losing battle against chickweed, lamb's quarters, creeping charlie, dandelions, couchgrass, old car axles, a decrepit black buggy with one wheel missing, pieces of iron and battered saucepans which might come in useful someday but never did, a broken babycarriage and two ruined armchairs with the springs hanging out and the upholstery torn and mildewed.* (The Diviners, p. 24)

Christie Logan is the first and greatest character from Morag's past and her first and greatest diviner, though it takes her most of her life to recognize this. He had fought in the First World War with Colin Gunn. He and Prin had offered to look after Morag when her parents died. Their kindness is speedily established for us:

> A little room. You might be safe in a place like that, if it was really yours. If they meant it.
> "I want to go to sleep," Morag says.
> And does that. They let her.
> *(The Diviners,* p. 25)

Margaret Laurence has made the Logans physically grotesque. Prin, short for Princess, is enormously fat, white, and lethargic, sitting in an armchair all day, looking "like a great big huge pear," eating jelly doughnuts. Christie with his sparse sandy hair, his bobbing Adam's apple, missing front

tooth, and outsized blue overalls, is a burning embarrassment
to Morag as she becomes aware that he is a clown-figure to the
town. He is in fact Manawaka's garbage man—by his own
choice. The kids jeer at him, calling him "The Scavenger," and
he replies by making foolish faces; Manawakans call the dump
"the nuisance grounds," and Christie always smells. Yet when
"the spiel" is on him, either from whiskey or in reaction to
jeering and insult, Christie is both preacher and prophet:

> "By their garbage shall ye know them," Christie
> yells, like a preacher, a clowny preacher. "I swear, by
> the ridge of tears and by the valour of my ancestors, I
> say unto you, Morag Gunn, lass, that by their bloody
> goddamn fucking garbage shall ye christly well know
> them. . . . They think muck's dirty. It's no more dirty
> than what's in their heads or mine.
>
> (*The Diviners*, p. 32)

Christie and Prin Logan are Grotesques, like Archipelago
and Doree in "The Perfume Sea," like Godman Piro, the
dwarf, or Hagar, ugly, monstrous, and old. Like these others
they are seeking spirits trapped in monstrously incongruous
flesh, but nonetheless capable of all of Everyman's range of
error or achievement. This is an important gallery among
Margaret Laurence's characters: her exaggeration is a way of
demonstrating that all flesh, young or old, ugly or beautiful, is
essentially incongruous to the potential of the spirit within.

The grotesque Prin, simple in every sense, is almost
entirely static, acted upon, not acting—a fool of God. Much
later in life, however, Morag realizes that Prin has actively
loved her. Christie Logan is a flaming, constant force in
Morag's life. He has given her a home and a love that the
reader is made immediately to see, but which the young Morag
cannot recognize because of her embarrassment at his
differentness. He also gives her the priceless gift of her
ancestors, back into the remote past. Inserted within the
Memorybank Movies are Christie's Tales, basic to the theme of
the ancestors in *The Diviners*, as well as another narrative

technique and another layer of density in its fabric. Because Christi's precious book, *The Clans and Tartans of Scotland*, gives no information about the Clan Gunn, he tells Morag tales of the great Pipr Gunn, who led the dispossessed crofters out of Scotland to Canada:

> Among all of them people there on the rocks, see, was a piper, and he was from the Clan Gunn, and it was many of the Gunns who lost their hearths and homes and lived wild on the stormy rocks there. And Piper Gunn, he was a great tall man, a man with the voice of drums and the heart of a child and the gall of a thousand and the strength of conviction. . . .
>
> Now Piper Gunn had a woman, and a strapping strong woman she was, with the courage of a falcon and the beauty of a deer and the warmth of a home and the faith of saints, and you may know her name. Her name, it was Morag. That was an old name, and that was the name Piper Gunn's woman went by, and fine long black hair she had, down to her waist, and she stood there beside her man on the rocky coast, and watched that ship come into the harbour in that place. And when the plank was down and the captain hailing the people there, Piper Gunn began to walk towards that ship and his woman Morag with him, and she with child, and he was still playing "The Gunns' Salute.". . . .
>
> And that was how all of them came to this country, all that bunch, and they ended up at the Red River, and that is another story. (*The Diviners*, p. 41)

Christie's tales as they are written in the text give the illusion of a storyteller and his oral tale. Long before, in her Somali translations, Margaret Laurence had worked to transcribe the tale to the page, distorting and violating its oral effects as little as possible. Now, she writes down the tales of the Bardic Christie, flown with red biddy, intoxicated with the past of the clans and declaiming in the strong rhythms of the Bible. And here the manner of the tales matches the teller, for it is easy to see—and to hear—Christie as he tells them.

The replaying of the past in Chapter Two takes Morag through her early school years, establishing her outsider-dom, the beginnings of her resentful toughness and the reasons for it. The chapter finishes with Morag adapting Christie's tale, retelling it to herself according to her own needs and taking heart from her sense of the first Morag's bravery. Margaret Laurence is beginning to show us the signs and signals of the writer in young Morag. She is also demonstrating the need of any individual for a historical past to feed into his present—and, that given, the process of adapting the past to the individual's own requirements:

> If they came to a forest, would this Morag there be scared? Not on your christly life. She would only laugh and say, *Forests cannot hurt me because I have the power and the second sight and the good eye and the strength of conviction.* (*The Diviners*, p. 42)

Chapter Three begins in the present, with the introduction of Maudie, A-Okay Smith, and their son Tom to Morag's contemporary circle. Maudie and A-Okay grew up in Toronto, but they have rejected the city and are determined to learn how to farm. To Morag they are sometimes naïve in their faith that they can re-establish an older and a simpler way of life, but they are also strong, and "However they might feel sometimes, now they were living and had to live as though their faith in their decision was not to be broken" (*The Diviners*, p. 47). They provide Morag with friendship and advice which she accepts or fends off with ironic good humour. But most important, they, in their late twenties, are intermediaries between Morag's generation and Pique's. They make another angle of vision possible for Morag. They are like a refracting glass whose surface illuminates areas she could not otherwise see.

A telephone call from Jules Tonnerre, Pique's father, is the first climactic peak in the process of the present. He is furious with Morag for letting Pique go, but he has at least seen her. Now the Memorybank Movies begin to feed more of Morag's past into her present. She is quite aware, however, of the self-structuring processes of memory: *"A popular misconception is that we can't change the past—everyone is constantly changing their own past, recalling it, revisiting it"*(*The Diviners*, p. 49). These scenes begin when Morag is twelve. They introduce Jules "Skinner" Tonnerre into the past action; they record more of Christie's tales, bringing Morag's ancestral past right up to the experience that Christie and Colin Gunn shared in the Battle of Bourlon Wood in the First World War. They establish the enchantment of words for Morag; she is charmed by the colours, sounds, and shapes that emanate from them when they are set next to one another and always, from the beginning, she asks repeatedly, "What means?"

These scenes also prepare the ground for the later insertions of the Tonnerre Tales, as Morag and Jules, together in school and already obscurely bonded by their recognition in each other of the everlasting outsider, tease and dare each other when they meet in the Nuisance Grounds:

> "Long time before my grandad, there's one Tonnerre they call Chevalier, and no man can ride like him and he is one helluva shot. My grandad, he tol' my dad about that guy, there."
> "What means *Chevalier*?"
> "Rider. It means Rider. Lazarus, he says so. Ah, what's it to *you*?" (*The Diviners*, p. 60)

The Memorybank Movies are very flexible to all kinds of narrative techniques, and Margaret Laurence adds variety to the elements through which they unfold their sequences: the dialogue Morag overhears from the teacher's room set down as in a written play; Ossian's poem describing the great chariot of Cuchullin which Christie reads to Morag as an antidote to Wordsworth; a piece of its original Gaelic; songs—a fragment of "O Canada," a Christmas hymn, and "The Maple Leaf Forever"; Morag's list of the contents of The Nuisance

Grounds; her first Christmas poem and Belloc's Christmas poem; her listed description of the chariot that Piper Gunn's Morag built in the new world; the Table of Contents of Christie's *The 60th Canadian Field Artillery Battery Book*; and, as she moves into adolescence, a fantasy-variation headed "Innerfilm" exposes various never-neverlands of Morag's dreams.

Chapter Four moves through the day of Royland's water-divining to the night of Pique's disturbing, yet also reassuring, telephone call. As she waits for Royland to take her to the Smiths', Morag moves from musings on the Coopers, who built this house and pioneered this land, to Catharine Parr Traill, the archetypal pioneer among Upper Canadian women. The ensuing conversations between Morag and Catharine constitute yet another variation in the narrative of *The Diviners*; having thought of her and consulted one of her books, Morag conjures her up. From time to time henceforth she engages in imaginary dialogues with Catharine. C.P.T., as Morag calls her, not only adds her particular dimension of the historical past to the total resonance of *The Diviners*, but she is also useful for varying the quiet flow of Morag's present. The Morag-Traill talks are ironic on Morag's part, calm with the confidence of achievement on Catharine's part, and they add both humour and a dimension of balance to Morag's present:

> What had Catharine said, somewhere, about emergencies?
> Morag loped over to the bookshelves which lined two walls of the seldom-used livingroom. Found the pertinent text.
>
> In cases of emergency it is folly to fold one's hands and sit down to bewail in abject terror. It is better to be up and doing.
> (*The Canadian Settlers' Guide*, 1855)
>
> *Morag:* Thank you, Mrs. Traill.

Catharine Parr Traill: That, my dear, was when we were at one time surrounded by forest fires which threatened the crops, fences, stock, stable, cabin, furniture and, of course, children. Your situation, if I may say so, can scarcely be termed comparable.

(*The Diviners*, p. 79)

After the telephone call from Winnipeg, which tells her that Pique is at the moment safe, and also that she has been to Manawaka, Morag's Memorybank moves us through her late high school years to the point of her leaving Manawaka for university. With its great elasticity, the Memorybank tells a great deal with a maximum of compression, moving chronologically from climax to climax. Most of the scenes focus on the hurts and humiliations that forced Morag's growth. We see and we understand her growing up tough, angry, determined to get away from everything that has wounded her—by which she means Manawaka and everyone in it—and never return.

The movies illuminate the miseries of her adolescence, but by no means for the sake of adolescent self-dramatizing and self-pity. Rather, everything that Morag remembers feeds into and points towards the interlocking parts of the strong self she has become. We are shown her growing obsession with words and her first self-conscious attempts at writing. And we are also shown the strong, first beginnings of her relationship with Jules Tonnerre. In "The Nuisance Grounds," her attempts at writing culminate in her refusal to be as vulnerable as she feels the publication of her story in the high school magazine would make her:

She has known for some time what she has to do, but never given the knowledge to any other person or thought that any person might suspect. Now it is as though a strong hand has been laid on her shoulders. Strong and friendly. But merciless.

(*The Diviners*, p. 99)

Morag is in her late teens and Jules has joined the army when they first make love in his shack down in the valley, just before he goes overseas with the Cameron Highlanders. The tragedy of Dieppe changes the town of Manawaka: "There are many dead who will not be buried in the Manawaka cemetery up on the hill where the tall spruces stand like dark angels. There are a great many families who now have fewer sons, or none" (*The Diviners*, p. 116). But Jules' name is not on the casualty lists, and as Morag lies awake thinking about him she remembers the stories he told her. Like Christie's Tales, these are inserted into the text as transcriptions of oral story-telling. Also, as do Christie's Tales for Morag, these tales, though Jules has professed to take them lightly, provide his identity through the generations. In both sets of tales, Margaret Laurence is not only affirming the importance of a past to the pride of a people, she is also demonstrating the way in which fact and the dramatic imagination of the story-teller combine to create and preserve the legends of the past. Like Christie's, Jules' tales centre around heroic figures: Rider Tonnerre and his great, mysterious white horse, Roi du Lac, leading the Métis to defeat the English and the Scotch who were threatening their lands; Rider Tonnerre and The Prophet, Riel, who, many years later on, shamed the Métis into defending their land; old Jules Tonnerre, Jules' grandfather, and his tale of the Battle of Batoche.

Reading the newspaper stories about Dieppe, Morag had wondered, "what is the true story? Is there any such thing?" Now, in Skinner's tales, the mixing of truth of fact and truth of the imagination is demonstrated:

Now this guy is—I guess you'd call him Prophet. He is like a prophet, see? And he has the power.
(The power?)
He can stop bullets—well, I guess he couldn't, but lots of people, there, they believed he could. And he has the sight, too. That means he can see through walls and he can see inside a man's head and see what people are thinking in there. He's Métis, but very

educated. How the hell he ever got to get that way, I wouldn't know.

(You're talking about Riel.)

Sure. But the books, they lie about him. I don't say Lazarus told the story the way it happened, but neither did the books and they're one hell of a sight worse because they made out that the guy was nuts.

(*The Diviners*, p. 119)

The final section of Memorybank Movies in "The Nuisance Grounds" dramatizes Morag's last year in Manawaka when she worked for Lachlan MacLachlan, editor and owner of the *Manawaka Banner*. The death of his son at Dieppe has crippled Lachlan, but he is still a wise newspaper man and from him Morag takes some healthy shake-ups:

"Those people know things it will take you the better part of your lifetime to learn, if ever. They are not very verbal people, but if you ever in your life presume to look down on them because you have the knack of words and they do not, then you do so at your eternal risk and peril. . . ."

"And for God's sake quit feeling set upon. You're not trapped. The doors are open."

(*The Diviners*, p. 126)

Morag's years in Manawaka are climaxed and closed by her involvement in two terrible events: she is sent by Lachlan to report on the death by fire of Piquette Tonnerre and her two children. This horror is the tragic, third-act finale to her experiences "Down in the Valley." And the terrified, desperate, self-induced abortion of Eva Winkler gives added strength to her one resolve: "Nothing—*nothing*—is going to endanger her chances of getting out of Manawaka. And on her own terms, not the town's" (*The Diviners*, p. 124). When Jules comes home again in the summer of 1945 he senses the strength of her resolve and her rejection of anything that might threaten her. Skinner tells her no "Tale" of Dieppe and the little that Morag can bear to hear fills her, not with its legendary quality, but with its murderous immediacy, the horror of present history.

"The Nuisance Grounds" ends with their parting:

"You want it so bad I can just about smell it on you. You'll get it, Morag."

"What's *it*?" . . .

He grins, but not in the old way, not con-spiratorially. Not quite hostile, but nearly. To him she is now on the other side of the fence. They inhabit the same world no longer. . . .

In the night, the train whistle says *Out There Out There Out There.*   (*The Diviners,* p. 134)

PART III, HALLS OF SION, CHAPTERS FIVE, SIX, SEVEN

"Halls of Sion," is similar in its shape to "The Nuisance Grounds." Its three chapters rise to a climax in Morag's present with Pique's return home. In the past they finish with the breaking up of another major (ten-year) section of Morag's life and her move to Vancouver. Like Part II, "Halls of Sion" also has an accelerating movement of increasing complexity and intensity so that its final chapter is a lengthy, fast-paced, complicated, and climactic interweaving of themes, persons, and events. In Chapter Five, Morag receives a postcard from Pique in Vancouver; in Chapter Seven, Pique is home from Vancouver and has broken off her relationship with Gord. The sections of counterpointed movement in Morag's past go from her arrival at university to her meeting with Brooke to her break with him after ten years of marriage. At the end of "Halls of Sion" Morag is on her way to Vancouver.

In this parallel movement between the lives of Morag and Pique, "Halls of Sion" begins to demonstrate the interweaving of the strands of the past and present for mother and daughter.

As the snapshots and Memorybank Movies of Part II established the past for us, Part III now begins to show the interaction of past and present, particularly after Pique's return. With Pique's return, also, the tempo of the narrative in the present can validly pick up—and does so. Essentially, Morag is still forced to be a watcher on the sidelines of Pique's life, but she is now also actively engaged in Pique's present, even if it be only in the wounding challenge of Pique's cry:

> "Why did you *have* me?"
> "I wanted you," Morag said, stunned.
> "For your own satisfaction, yes. You never thought of him, or of me." (*The Diviners*, p. 193)

Morag also becomes active in her role as comforter of Gord when Pique feels she must break away from him. She has no power of her own to move out of her becalmed state, but she is given an active part in the present again by Pique's needs for reassurance and demands for justification.

Chapter Five moves from Pique's postcard and Morag's musings about Brooke Skelton's picture in the newspaper into the Memorybank Movies that take her from Manawaka into university, into her friendship with Ella Gerston and her family, and then to the brink of her marriage with Professor Brooke Skelton of the English Department. That Jules Tonnerre is Pique's father has been firmly established in "The Nuisance Grounds." Brooke Skelton is newly introduced as Morag looks at the paper:

> There was the picture of Brooke. Telling about his new appointment. Not just Head of an English Department, not now. President of a university. Well, well.
> *My God, what a handsome man he still is.*
> Another shed skin of another life. And it began happening again, again, as it had been doing for years, and perhaps the film would never end until she did. (*The Diviners*, p. 140)

Perhaps the most difficult challenge Margaret Laurence faced as she wrote *The Diviners* begins now, as she must fill in the character of Brooke Skelton and his relation to Morag. The reader has long since been caught up in the situation and the unanswered questions having to do with the Morag-Pique-Jules triangle. Furthermore, "The Nuisance Grounds" established the young Jules Tonnerre, both in himself and in relation to the young Morag. In a very real sense, Brooke is a latecomer to the narrative—and he is also, obviously, a loser in Morag's life. Quite soon, Brooke also comes to represent an orientation to life that is quite alien to anything that Morag has known, or that she can possibly adapt to permanently. He is very much a part of the Establishment of society. Underneath an impressive façade, he is as insecure as Morag herself, and he is woefully lacking in the ability or the desire to imagine her needs and potentials beyond her physical self. All his drive and ambition focus on moving rung by rung upwards through the university hierarchy. Morag was always an outsider to the social structure in Manawaka; and as she grew up, her hurt and resentment made her both consciously and defensively determined to preserve her own differentness. Furthermore, her precious friendship with Ella Gerston began simultaneously with her awareness of Brooke at university. Under the wing of Ella's mother she has begun her theoretical education in world literature—and in socialist and communist ideology:

> Ella's Ma has adopted Morag in some way or other, and is going to give her the same benefits as her own daughters receive. Cannily she leaves the HCPSU (History of the Communist Party in the Soviet Union) until later on. For now, Dostoevsky, Tolstoy, Chekhov, Turgenev. (*The Diviners*, p. 151)

We see Brooke entirely in terms of Morag's memory; her life with him is a "shed skin," and she is all too well aware that neither she nor Brooke, in the ten years of their marriage, ever knew each other as whole people: "We were acting out each other's fantasies." Compared to any of the major characters in the books, Brooke is both remote and two-dimensional—but this is the whole point.

It is perfectly logical that Brooke should have a great glamour for the young Morag. He seems to her to *be*, and he certainly represents to her everything she wants, all the prestige, the security, the intellectual fulfilment and the glamour that she left Manawaka to search for, but didn't dare hope to find. Furthermore, their mutual sexual attraction is important and convincingly portrayed. From the start of their relationship, however, warnings are built into the text: Brooke's calling Morag "Little one," the condescension of his attitudes to her, his own deep-rooted insecurity and, because of that, his unwillingness to have a child; and always, underneath, the final time-bomb: not only does he not take Morag's writing as seriously as she must take it, he also feels obscurely, but definitely, threatened by it.

Perhaps their basic incompatibility is from the start made too obvious to the reader. Given the strength of will and the drive to write previously established in Morag, the reader finishes "Halls of Sion" amazed that such superficiality could hold her for ten years. On the other hand, the long accumulation of tension between Brooke and Morag does make the final violence of her breakaway and the reactionary "rightness" for her of her affair with Jules Tonnerre completely believable. There is also the matter of historic time: Brooke's kind of formal, mandarin academic is compatible to the decade of the fifties, when the gates of the university ivory-tower had hardly been threatened. In the seventies, it is even believable that, given the toughness to survive the shatterings of the system, a Brooke Skelton would indeed have achieved the dangerous eminence of a university presidency.

More basically important to *The Diviners* than Brooke's credibility, however, is the account we get in "Halls of Sion" of Morag's painful birth into a writer. Margaret Laurence's Manawaka works touch, echo, and relate to the works of Willa Cather at many points, but nowhere as hauntingly as in this novel, where Morag Gunn, writer, is impelled, laboriously and inexorably, to exercise her talent. *Song Of The Lark*, the story of Thea Kronborg of Moonstone, Colorado, who becomes a great Wagnerian soprano, is Willa Cather's portrait of a woman as artist. Harsanyi, Thea Kronborg's teacher, says, "Every artist makes himself born. It is very much harder than the other time and longer." And this is precisely the process that is dramatized for us as Morag Gunn wrestles to set down her first character, Lilac Stonehouse of the terrifying innocence:

> Lilac's staggering naïveté is never presented as anything but harmful, and in fact it damages not only herself but others. Innocence may well be the eighth deadly sin. . . .
>
> She knows more about Lilac than Lilac knows about herself, but how to convey this? It is being written in the third person, but from Lilac's viewpoint, and as this is a limited one, people have to be communicated to the reader solely through their words and acts, which Lilac often does not understand. . . .

Sometimes she forgets that time, outside, is passing.

> This afternoon she has forgotten, because Lilac has aborted herself in a way that Morag recalls from long ago. And yet it is not Eva for whom Morag experiences pain now—it is Lilac only, at this moment. . . .
>
> Odd—if you had a friend who had just aborted herself, causing chaos all around and not only to herself, no one would be surprised if you felt upset, anxious, shaken. It is no different with fiction—more so, maybe, because Morag has felt Lilac's feelings. The blood is no less real for being invisible to the external eye.   (*The Diviners*, pp. 184-188)

Close to the end of *Song Of The Lark*, Willa Cather says: "Artistic growth is, more than anything else, a refining of the sense of truthfulness. The stupid believe that to be truthful is easy; only the artist, the great artist, knows how difficult it is." Willa Cather distanced herself from her heroine and freed herself from inhibitions about the discussion of her own art by making Thea Kronborg a singer. Because Morag Gunn is a writer, Margaret Laurence has no such distance. Never, through Morag, does she speak of "art"; Morag speaks of her writing as her "trade," her "work," bed-rock terms, the way she makes her living. What we are witnessing, however, is precisely the process that, in her day and in the circumstances of her fiction, Willa Cather felt free to proclaim as "art." We are shown the process of Morag Gunn's writing her first novel, *Spear of Innocence*, laboriously seeking for the truth of conception and the matching words that will bring Lilac Stonehouse into being in her book. As her character is born and assumes life, so do we see Morag coming into being as a writer. The process is exhilarating, often painful, but always *necessary*.

Morag's memory in "Halls of Sion" also gives us, stage-by-stage, the process of creation from the time when she began to write ("almost unexpectedly, although Lilac has been in her mind for some time") through a first rejection of the manuscript to the exhilaration of a publisher's acceptance of her book and the drudgery of its rewriting:

> This rewriting is a thousand miles from the first setting down. No half-lunatic sense of possession, of being possessed by the thing. In fact, this is much easier, but without exhilaration. . . .
>
> Morag realizes, with some surprise, that she is able to defend her own work. Also, it is a relief to be able to discuss it, no holds barred, with no personal emotional connotations in the argument. Only when the process is completed does she see that it has been like exercising muscles never before used, stiff and painful at first, and then later, filled with the knowledge that this part of herself really is there.
>
> (*The Diviners*, p. 212)

Only at this point, with this much work gone through, is she able to say to Brooke, "I know you know a lot about novels. But I know something, as well. Different from reading or teaching." Then the gratuitous sarcasm of his rejoinder triggers action—violent action, in contrast to the deference to his opinions that the earlier Morag had always imposed upon herself.

As deep a reason for Morag's alienation from Brooke as the fact of her writing is his unwillingness to have a child. At first he postpones the decision; later Morag knows that he will never agree—he is too insecure in himself to wish to share responsibility for a child. Later still she knows that she will never bring up the matter again, and that, in fact, she does not wish to bear his child now. Their marriage is sterile and Brooke wants it so:

> "Does it seem like the kind of world, to you," he says, "to bring children into?"
> To that, there is no answer. None. No, it does not seem like the kind of world, etcetera. But she wants children all the same. Why? Something too primitive to be analyzed? Something which needs to proclaim itself, against all odds? Or only the selfishness of wanting someone born of your flesh, someone related to you? (*The Diviners,* p. 201)

Morag goes back to Manawaka because Prin is dying. At her funeral, standing beside Christie, singing "Jerusalem the Golden," Prin's favourite hymn, Morag is desperately aware of the wreck of her marriage:

> Those halls of Sion, The Prince is ever in them. What had Morag expected, those years ago, marrying Brooke? Those selfsame halls?
> And now here, in this place, the woman who brought Morag up is lying dead, and Morag's mind, her attention, has left Prin. *Help me, God; I'm frightened of myself.* (*The Diviners,* p. 207)

Blocked, hurt, and frustrated by Brooke in both her potentialities for creativity and giving life, Morag tramps the streets in panic, and meets Jules Tonnerre, who has become a travelling country and western singer. She takes him home with her. When Brooke sarcastically insults him, "I thought it was supposed to be illegal to give liquor to Indians," Jules leaves and Morag rushes after him. She stays with him for three weeks and he leaves her free to have his child if she wishes. Then she goes west to Vancouver.

PART IV, RITES OF PASSAGE, CHAPTERS EIGHT, NINE, TEN

In the overall shape of *The Diviners*, Part IV, "Rites of Passage," begins the long series of curves that flow together toward the novel's gradual resolution. The first lines, as Morag walks by the river, carry their signal of the inextricable mingling of past and present that Part IV unfolds: "On the opposite bank, upriver a little from A-Okay's place, the light-leafed willows and tall solid maples were like ancestors, carrying within themselves the land's past" (*The Diviners*, p. 235). In the present, throughout this section, Morag receives a series of reassurances, the first of these from Pique and her new man, Dan, who understand her loneliness and her shamed resentment of their relationship more readily than she would have believed possible:

> Silence. Then astonishment. Pique had taken one of her hands and Dan the other.
> "We thought that was what it was," Pique said, "but we couldn't say it unless you said it. And, like, we're aware you're alone, Ma. But in other ways you aren't. You know?" (*The Diviners*, p. 238)

Pique and Dan move out of Morag's house to live at the Smith's, with whom they plan to raise and sell horses. They leave Morag with understanding and a feeling of peace.

At the beginning of Chapter Nine, Pique is still letting her old resentment against Morag show, but she is also communicating with her mother. Morag, for her part, is realizing the paradox of her search for a safe island for herself, her daughter, or anyone else:

> *I've made an island. Are islands real? A-Okay and Maudie, and now Dan, are doing the same. But if they do raise horses, they'll have to sell them to the very people they despise. And, Morag Gunn, who rails against the continuing lies of the media, does not, it will be noticed, establish her own hand-set press. Islands are unreal.*   (*The Diviners*, p. 292)

As she goes out with Royland in the boat after Pique's departure, Morag is uplifted and reassured by the sight of a great blue heron. The description of this bird functions in *The Diviners* as an epic simile, flashing its meaning back over what has gone before and forward across what is to come. It is an image of acceptance and affirmation, central to the resolution of *The Diviners* and to the final and cumulative meaning of all the Manawaka novels:

> Then she saw the huge bird. It stood close to shore, its tall legs looking fragile although in fact they were very strong, its long neck and long sharp beak bent towards the water, searching for fish, its feathers a darkbright blue. A Great Blue Heron. Once populous in this part of the country. Now rarely seen.
>
> Then it spotted the boat, and took to flight. A slow unhurried takeoff, the vast wings spreading, the slender elongated legs gracefully folding up under the creature's body. Like a pterodactyl, like an angel, like something out of the world's dawn. The soaring and measured certainty of its flight. Ancient-seeming, unaware of the planet's rocketing changes. The sweeping serene wings of the thing, unknowing that it was speeding not only towards individual

The Diviners 157

death but probably towards the death of its kind. The mastery of the heron's wings could be heard, a rush of wind, the wind of its wings, before it mounted high and disappeared into the trees above a bywater of the river. . . .

That evening, Morag began to see that here and now was not, after all, an island. Her quest for islands had ended some time ago, and her need to make pilgrimages had led her back here.

(*The Diviners*, p. 292)

In the present of Chapter Ten, it is autumn. The leaves have turned colour, the swallows have gone, Morag is working well, "the words not having to be dredged up out of the caves of her mind, but rushing out in a spate so that her hand could not keep up with them." A-Okay and Dan have bought their first horse, a palamino gelding, and heckled and advised by Royland, they have made practical plans for making some money and for learning farming seriously. Only Pique is unsettled and uncertain:

Pique picked up her guitar and began to sing. Around her, there was an area of silence, as though all of them, all in this room, here, now, wanted to touch and hold her, and could not, did not dare tamper with her aloneness. She began to sing one of Jules's songs, the song for Lazarus. Her voice never faltered, although she was crying. (*The Diviners*, p. 335)

In "Halls of Sion" the Memorybank Movies move through Morag's pregnancy and Pique's birth, through Pique's growing-up to age fifteen when, finally settled on the farm in Ontario, Jules Tonnerre visited them once again and sang his songs for Pique.

The need to survive and then to grow had impelled Morag to reject, first Manawaka, and then the cocoon of unreality that her marriage with Brooke came to be. In Vancouver, pregnant, frightened, still distraught because of what she sees as her betrayal of Brooke, and still totally uncertain that she can make a living by writing for herself and her child, Morag knows that she must go on, that she cannot go back:

> Insane to have come here. Would have been better to have gone back to Manawaka. Christie needs her, and she needs a home for herself and her child, when it is born. But there is no way she can return to Manawaka. If she is to have a home, she must create it. (*The Diviners*, p. 239)

Morag's years in Vancouver and Pique's early years are presented as a fast, kaleidoscopic gallery of brief encounters and temporary relationships. Some of the portraits are two-dimensional only—neither in fact nor in her memory did Hank Masterson, Harold, or Chas have any depth-reality to Morag, though Chas is closer to a presentment of evil personified than any character that Margaret Laurence has ever drawn.

The Manawaka works begin to flow together through Morag's encounter in Vancouver with Julie Kazlik:

> "Really? My God, how many people from town must be here?"
>
> "Thousands, probably," Julie says in her old slapdash way. "We all head west, kiddo. We think it'll be heaven on earth—no forty below in winter, no blastfurnace in summer, and mountains to look at, not just grain elevators. So we troop out to the Coast, and every time we meet someone from back home we fall on their necks and weep. Stupid, eh?"
>
> Neither of them think it is stupid. You Can't Go Home Again, said Thomas Wolfe. Morag wonders now if it may be the reverse which is true. You have to go home again, in some way or other. This concept cannot yet be looked at. (*The Diviners*, p. 248)

Maggie Tefler, Morag's landlady and employer during her

pregnancy, is real enough in her greasy, Sairy Gampish self-righteousness. And Fan Brady, "Danseuse," also known as Princess Eureka, Snake Dancer, who "Dances with a Real Live Python," is another memorable variant among Margaret Laurence's gallery of Grotesques. Fan cultivates her superficial strangeness like a garden and wears it like an armour, to match the only world she sees around her and to protect the hurts and fears—and the essential goodness—of her inner self:

> She wears her flaming auburn hair in an odd assortment of ringlets, frizz and spitcurls like a calendar girl from the Mary Pickford era, and yet on Fan this coiffure doesn't look old-fashioned. Her face isn't beautiful—it isn't even pretty. In fact, facially, she rather resembles a monkey. She is well aware of this, and doesn't give a damn. When she has applied her false eyelashes, green eyeshadow, orange lipstick, and multitudinous other bits of makeup, she looks weird. But from a distance, possibly, and under coloured lights, there would be certain circus sequinned splendour about her. (*The Diviners*, p. 253)

Fan dances with her Python, even loves the snake and is inconsolable when he dies; Pique is unafraid also; only Morag is terrified. Knowing Fan, Morag is appalled and fascinated by the intertwinings of life and fiction, for Fan is "almost like looking at some distorted and older but still recognizable mirror-image" of Lilac Stonehouse: "there is a sense in which Fan *has* that same terrifying innocence, expressed in different ways." And of course, Margaret Laurence's ambivalent symbolism is clearly marked for us to read. Fan Brady is an Eve, both long-lost through the circumstances that destined her, and yet, in the deepest sense, forever incorruptible, grotesquely dancing with a harmless, drugged serpent.

The Vancouver years climax when Pique is five years old and Jules Tonnerre stays with them for two months. His young brother, Paul, has been killed in a mysterious accident up north, while working as guide for two American tourists. His

sister, Valentine, is sick and despairing over Paul's death; Jules
has come to Vancouver to persuade her to go into hospital for
treatment. Of the whole family, only his brother, Jacques, on a
farm near Galloping Mountain, seems settled and content:
"He doesn't waste his time in brawls, like Lazarus used to, and
I've had my share of that, too, I guess" (*The Diviners*, p. 279).

As always, Jules and Morag are bound together by the
strength of their passion and, on Morag's side at least, by her
deep recognition of kinship to Jules, both in the hurts he has
been born to and in her respect for his aloneness. Added to
that, they are now bound by Pique: " 'Sure Morag,' he says.
'She's yours, all right. But she's mine, too, eh?' " (*The
Diviners*, p. 277).

Their unity as a family is marked and sealed by Jules'
singing to them his "Ballad of Jules Tonnerre," the story of his
grandfather and the Battle of Batoche. Morag has known that
she will always live with Jules' sporadic rejection and
resentment towards her, because to him she represents the
dispossessors of his people. To herself, she is also one of the
dispossessed. She now sees that in the song, Jules has been
able to sing the pride in his people and the pity for them that he
could never bring himself to say:

> He took his Cross, and he took his gun,
> Went back to the place where he'd begun.
> He lived on drink and he lived on prayer,
> But the heart was gone from Jules Tonnerre.
>
> Still, he lived his years and he raised his son,
> Shouldered his life till it was done;
> His voice is one the wind will tell
> In the prairie valley that's called Qu'Appelle.
>
> They say the dead don't always die;
> They say the truth outlives the lie—
> The night wind calls their voices there,
> The Métis men, like Jules Tonnerre.
>
> (*The Diviners*, p. 283).

Chapter Nine's long sequence of Memorybank Movies, beginning after the great blue heron's flight had brought a certain peace to Morag, takes her life and Pique's through eight years in England. After Jules leaves them in Vancouver and Fan Brady loses her job, Morag takes Pique to England, partly to be close to a lively literary scene, "because of a fantasy—Morag getting to know dozens of other writers, with whom she would have everything in common" (*The Diviners*, p. 294). During the Vancouver years her second novel, *Prospero's Child*, had been accepted by three publishers, in Canada, the United States, and England. In London, Morag works mornings for Jeremy Sampson in his Agonistes Bookshop; at night after Pique is in bed, she works at *Jonah*, her third novel. The picture of these years is as somber as the "weak graylight of the morning" through which Morag walks to the Agonistes Bookshop. Morag's life is lonely and dominated by anxiety—about Pique, about her finances, about her ability to get her own work done. Nevertheless, she tells Pique tales of Christie Logan and Lazarus Tonnerre which will give her child a heritage of ancestors as Christie's tales had given hers to Morag. She puts off going to Scotland, to Sutherland where her people came from, though when Christie writes her about it, she answers "Soon." Morag's affair with Dan McRaith, the painter from Crombruach in Ross shire, is the only leavener of these years. Like herself, McRaith is always essentially a stranger in London; he comes down, away from his wife Bridie, and the seven children that are her life, and paints in London until he can stand it no longer. Then he goes back to Crombruach where his best work is always done.

Among the characters of *The Diviners*, Dan McRaith has a low-keyed quality that matches Morag's own. Margaret Laurence is extraordinarily successful at presenting Dan and establishing the combination of friendship and sexual attraction that he and Morag feel for each other. They meet as equals, and though Morag feels intermittently the frustrations of being used by Dan, of demeaning herself by being his mistress, and of guilt about his wife, she also knows that, "If he were here all the time . . . she would become impatient with

him, resentful of anyone's constant presence." Given the
double demands of Pique and her work, Morag comes to
accept in herself not only the necessity for being alone and so
free, but also, ultimately, her absolute need for freedom.
When she visits Crombruach with Pique, Bridie and the
children are made real to her, and McRaith explains the importance of this place to him: "When I look out there, I see the
firth. It's the place that's important to me. The surrounding
circumstances—well, they have happened and they are here"
(*The Diviners,* p. 317). This trip results in two important
recognitions for Morag: she knows that her love affair with Dan
is over but that their friendship is a solid bond between them;
and she accepts that her need to search for her ancestors in
Sutherland has disappeared:

> "Away over there is Sutherland, Morag Dhu, where
> your people came from. When do you want to drive
> there?" . . .
> "I thought I would have to go. But I guess I don't
> after all." . . .
> "I don't know that I can explain. It has to do with
> Christie. The myths are my reality. Something like
> that. And also, I don't need to go there because I
> know now what it was I had to learn here." . . .
> "It's a deep land here, all right," Morag says. "But
> it's not mine, except a long long way back. I always
> thought it was the land of my ancestors, but it is not."
> "What is, then?"
> "Christie's real country. Where I was born."
> (*The Diviners*, p. 318)

There are many climaxes in the Memorybank Movies of
The Diviners, because it is of the very essence of Morag, the
writer, that she remembers her past as stories and that these
take on the shape of the rising action that is contained in them.
But the scenes of Morag's return to Manawaka for Christie's
death and burial build to a greater climax than any of the
others. They communicate a massive compound of love, pity,

and mourning, shot through with the relieving incongruity of laughter. Before Christie dies, Morag finally has time to say the words she needs to say to him: "Christie—I used to fight a lot with you, Christie, but you've been my father to me." Christie answers, "Well—I'm blessed."

Christie Logan's funeral is one of the greatest of scenes in Margaret Laurence's work. It is comparable in its power to the scene of Hagar in hospital, daring Mr. Troy to sing "Old Hundred" for her, and then being released into the magnificence of her "Pride was my wilderness" confession. It is also comparable to that scene in the technique of its build-up, the almost meaningless conventionality of the funeral juxtaposed to the half-ridiculous, half-noble incongruity of the piper—and out of the amalgam, a double issue, an unforgettable picture and unforgettable prose:

> He swings the pipes up, and there is the low mutter of the drones. Then he begins, pacing the hillside as he plays. And Morag sees, with the strength of conviction, that this is Christie's true burial.
>
> *And Piper Gunn, he was a great tall man, with the voice of drums and the heart of a child, and the gall of a thousand, and the strength of conviction.*
>
> The piper plays "The Flowers of the Forest," the long-ago pibroch, the lament for the dead, over Christie Logan's grave. And only now is Morag released into her mourning. (*The Diviners*, p. 329)

The movement from this great climax of the past in Chapter Nine back to the present in Chapter Ten marks an emotional levelling out, a consolidation for Morag. In her present she is moving on through a series of affirmations, resolutions, and acceptances: at the beginning of Chapter Ten she has her last imaginary conversation with Catharine Parr Traill and defends what she, Morag, has managed to do in her life:

> One thing I'm going to stop doing, though, Catharine. I'm going to stop feeling guilty that I'll

> never be as hardworking or knowledgeable or all-round terrific as you were. . . . And yet in my way I've worked damn hard, and I haven't done all I would've liked to do, but I haven't folded up like a paper fan, either. . . . This place is some kind of a garden, nonetheless, even though it may be only a wildflower garden.   (*The Diviners*, p. 331)

Here also she accepts Pique's restlessness and the necessity for her—as for all of the young—to find her own way: " 'It'll be a-okay,' she said finally, not knowing whether it would be or not, but praying" (*The Diviners*, P. 335).

As the Memorybank Movie "Beulah Land" begins in the time immediately after Christie's death, Morag is at the bottom of her emotional pit, "like a zombie or a sleepwalker." She only comes out of her depression and stasis when, by chance, she reads an advertisement for the sale of an eighty-acre farm at McConnell's Landing: "Land, A river. Log house nearly a century old, built by great pioneering couple, Simon and Sarah Cooper. History. Ancestors" (*The Diviners*, p. 338). The next three years of settling and of writing her fourth novel, *Shadow of Eden*, based on Piper Gunn and the trek of the Highlanders to Canada, climax in Pique's unhappiness at school where she has been called "a dirty half-breed" and in Jules' culminating and final visit to them. He sings his songs to Morag and Pique, the old one for Jules and new ones for his sister, Piquette, and for Lazarus, his father. On this visit Jules finally tells Pique the things that she must know but which are not Morag's right or responsibility to tell—about the fire and about the deaths of Paul and Val, who "died of booze and speed, on the streets of Vancouver": " 'Too many have died,' he says. 'Too many, before it was time. I don't aim to be one of them. And I don't aim for you to be, neither' " (*The Diviners*, p. 351). He also points Pique towards his brother Jacques and the place on Galloping Mountain as a kind of area of security and hope out of all the drifting and loss of his family.

Chapter Ten and "Rites of Passage" end on Morag and Jules' acceptance of what they have been to each other and what they have each been to their daughter. The culmination of their relationship is peace, marked by the strange coincidence of Morag's finding that the hunting knife Christie gave her long ago belonged to old Lazarus. She exchanges it for the plaid pin that Jules has, the pin that John Shipley had traded to Lazarus. "Fair trade," said Jules of the exchange of tokens, and all their relationship, Morag realizes, has indeed been a fair trade—of their need for each other and their mutual reassurance. Morag identifies the crest from her *Clans and Tartans of Scotland*, recognizes and accepts the mysterious gift:

> *My Hope Is Constant In Thee*. It sounds like a voice from the past. Whose voice, though? Does it matter? It does not matter. What matters is that the voice is there, and that she has heard these words which have been given to her. And will not deny what has been given. *Gainsay Who Dare*.   (*The Diviners*, p. 353)

The token of the plaid pin joins *The Diviners* to *The Stone Angel* and Morag Gunn to Hagar Shipley, whose shield and buckler had been the motto and the war-cry of her clan. Hagar used them defiantly; Morag interprets them as mysterious supports. Again the distant past curves into the present of *The Diviners*, bringing a new significance to old words according to the need and the comprehension of the inheritor. Morag's life has forced pain on her, but also growth. Her "Rites of Passage" as woman *and* writer are now complete.

Part V, called "The Diviners," is, like Part I, very brief—a second moving west for Pique, and for Morag a peace and acceptance that had not been possible for her in Pique's earlier departure. That first leaving and her accompanying anxiety had set all the Memorybank Movies of her past in train. Now, she has finally seen all the patterns of her own life unfolding from an ancestral past over which she had no control, through the moments of her own life over which she has had much control and for which she now can accept responsibility without disabling guilt, and on to the lives of the inheriting generation, over which, as she now sees, she neither has nor should

have control. Before Pique leaves, she sings her song to
Morag, thus completing the song-cycle of the Tonnerre
generations, from old Jules' Ballad of Batoche, through Jules'
songs of Lazarus and Piquette, to Pique's own song. She must
now go back to the land on Galloping Mountain:

> Ah, my valley and my mountain, they're the same
> My living places, and they never will be tame
> When I think how I was born
> I can't help but being torn
> But the valley and the mountain hold my name.
> The valley and the mountain hold my name.

Then silence. Pique could not speak until Morag
did, and Morag could not speak for a while. The hurts
unwittingly afflicted upon Pique by her mother, by
circumstances—Morag had agonized over these
often enough, almost as though, if she imagined
them sufficiently, they would prove to have been
unreal after all. But they were not unreal. Yet Pique
was not assigning any blame—that was not what it
was all about. And Pique's journey, although at this
point it might feel to her unique, was not unique.
                    (*The Diviners*, p. 360)

Beyond a certain boundary which is not ours to set, we cannot
know our children. Morag, in her relationship to Pique, has
been totally convincing in her hesitancy, her vulnerability, and
her sense of a largely mysterious other-being in her daughter;
now by her acceptance of Pique's otherness we are, rightly,
reassured.

Morag's journey away from Manawaka had been
determined by her own resentment and sense of loss, and by
the toughness and determination these had bred in her.
Pique's second journey takes her back to her own people,
freely, without resentment towards Morag, or towards Jules,
or towards the past. Morag had rebelled and fought convention

and all the establishments of society in order to have her child and to do her work, her twin necessities. Pique is free to find her own, particular work. She is an inheritor of "Diviners," both Morag and Jules; in her carrying on of the old songs—and in her own, new song—she has already begun to carry the responsibility of being a "Diviner" herself.

Jules has throat cancer; Morag sees him one last time and then his singing partner, Billy Joe, brings her word of his death: " 'He didn't wait for it,' Billy Joe said." He brings Morag the knife, which she passes on to Pique; the plaid pin, the second symbol of Pique's inheritance, will come to her when Morag is dead. Morag's relationship to Jules Tonnerre is tragically finished and Morag's mourning for him continues, but her relationship to him, and Pique's, had resolved itself on his last visit to them. Morag's anxiety about Pique is stilled into an acceptance that is not a passive endurance, but is a dynamic understanding. Through the novel the progress of Morag herself has been very like the moving of Milton's Samson, from stasis and blindness to "calm of mind, all passion spent." Morag is finally able to accept herself, without the debilitating feelings of guilt that have always haunted her—and there always remains her work to be done. Royland's failure to divine his well is the final episode of the book, bringing its closing affirmation to Morag:

> "It's something I don't understand, the divining," Royland said slowly, "and it's not something that everybody can do, but the thing I don't usually let on about is that quite a few people can learn to do it. You don't have to have the mark of God between your eyebrows. Or if you do, quite a few people have it. You didn't know that, did you?" . . .
>
> The inheritors. Was this, finally and at last, what Morag had always sensed she had to learn from the old man? She had known it all along, but not really known. The gift, or portion of grace, or whatever it was, was finally withdrawn, to be given to someone else.

> "This that's happened to me—" Royland said, "it's
> not a matter for mourning."
> "I see that now," Morag said.
>
> > (*The Diviners*, p. 369)

There are many diviners, she sees—Christie, Lazarus, Jules, Royland, and now, perhaps, Pique. They function through many means and media. "The gift or portion of grace" is translated into words or deeds by an act that is essentially an act of love, indistinguishable from worshipping, whether it issue in a book or a newly divined well. The individual may lose the gift, but grace itself is not exhaustible.

> *Look ahead into the past, and back into the future,*
> *until the silence. . . .*
> > Morag returned to the house, to write the remain-
> > ing private and fictional words, and to set down her
> > title.   (*The Diviners*, p. 370)

That title, of the work that has been in preparation, can now only be "The Diviners."

The Diviners culminates and closes the circle of the Manawaka works. It is a complex and a profound novel, an exploration of the meaning of a life, a quest, and finally the affirmation of a life's meaning. Its pattern is a diagram of the interweaving of the past into the present and on into the future. The shape of its flowing together of past and present is that of the ancient Yoruba symbol of the endless continuum of time, the serpent swallowing his tail. Repeatedly, Margaret Laurence demonstrates that the continuum moves inexorably, but she also demonstrates that the present and the future are not relentlessly and totally predetermined by the past. They may be modified and ameliorated by the force of faith, acted out in love. This perception is the final statement of affirmation in what is a profoundly hopeful book: the past is inevitably a part of us, but not the dead hand of the past; rather, by faith, by grace, translated into acts of love, the inheritors may inch upward, though still within the enclosing coils of the present.

The Diviners is the epic of Morag Gunn, whose story is contained within a structure as complex as that of a classical epic, and one that incorporates many of the traditional epic techniques. Sometimes playfully, but cumulatively in a very serious way, we see the incorporation of the epic conventions: the stories of heroes and their battles, the lists and heightened descriptions, the contained epic, the transposition of the oral into the written—and one magnificent epic simile. Technically, this novel moves much further on in the complexity of its structure from the "voices and pictures" orchestration of *The Fire-Dwellers*. But in *The Diviners*, to achieve her final pattern, Margaret Laurence has gone back to the epic, that most spacious of all literary genres, yet one whose final effectiveness depends upon the containment of its variety within a tight structure.

As by tradition the epic manifests the fulfilment of prophecy, so *The Diviners* fulfils the early promise of Morag Gunn's talent. Explicit for Morag and implicit for all men and women is the "Contained Epic"—the search for home. This strong theme moves through Christie's tales, Jules' songs, and Morag's life as a journeying stranger. It begins its resolution in Scotland, where she realizes that her real land is Christie's land, and fans out finally from the simile of the great blue heron in flight to the recognition of a cosmological design, beyond time and space as we know them, containing man as one of its myriad interlocking patterns.

Throughout the novel, Morag's attitudes to the natural world have been markedly different from Hagar's or Rachel's or Stacey's. The first three novels are dense with images of animals and birds, but these are used to set their speakers apart from nature. When, for instance, Rachel sees herself as an outlandish birdlike creature as she does repeatedly; or when Stacey dreams of a quiet place where she will "live in the light of the morning," nature is most definitely separated from mankind. It is an Other World in which man exists as onlooker, or marauder, or conqueror, but never as brother-creature. In contrast, Morag sees herself as living within nature. The animal and bird images are markedly absent from her voice.

Instead she watches the birds and identifies with their problems of family-raising—unrepentantly anthropomorphic, as she willingly admits. Her wish for Pique and Dan, A-Okay and Maudie, is that they learn to use the land without setting it up as their adversary and so doing battle with it. Morag's conversations with Catharine Parr Traill have a significance in this context beyond the sense of the past, or the comedy, that they add to *The Diviners*. Catharine Traill was a gifted and an indefatigible naturalist; of all the pioneer women who left records, her works alone show a grateful and a joyful acceptance of her natural environment and a constant, enquiring intelligence about its best uses by man.

Morag's setting of herself within nature, not as an alien to it, and her calling upon Catharine Traill as her "saint" reflect, of course, the concerns and fears of the present about ecology and conservation. But more than that, and signified throughout by Royland's mysterious gift of finding the water underneath the earth, *The Diviners* makes a cumulative statement about the mysterious presence, not only of grace, but also of design within and through all the universe and its creatures. Hagar found her freedom almost in spite of herself in a journey through her past that was unconsciously Christian-sacramental in its design; Rachel and Stacey project their images of man on God and address him as remote, inscrutable, terrifying, or sometimes as vulnerable as themselves. When she was young, Morag rejected the vengeful, Old Testament of God, but "Jesus was O.K." Her final acceptance and affirmation comes from her maturity's understanding of all the diviners—scapegoats, seers, and agents of grace. The novel ends, and the Manawaka cycle ends, with a resolution of the ME and the NOT-ME into the humility of an acceptance of a place within the ALL.

It is a profoundly religious novel and its final assertion speaks for a Miltonic Eternal Providence. In fact, the echoes of *Paradise Lost* are strong throughout, both in its foundation-fabric and in its precise details. The farm gates clang shut behind Morag and she loses Eden. Margaret Laurence has always written of the dispossessed—and, on her works' deepest level, the dispossessed of Eden. She perceives all men and women, not as pawns in a cosmic battle of Good and Evil, of Darkness and Light, but more puzzling than that, as damaging and destroying one another in the grip of some mysterious Primal Darkness. The miracle is that they are also, often tragically, sometimes joyously, but always stubbornly, stumbling onward towards the Light. Morag's final understanding, the energy of her acceptance, is her "Paradise Regained"—and by implication, Everyman's. When she wrote *The Diviners*, Margaret Laurence was not aware of the lines that Catharine Traill, when she was well into her nineties, quoted as her statement of faith: "Something gathers up the fragments, and nothing is lost" (*Pearls and Pebbles*, p. 241). At the end, Morag's faith is very close to Catharine Traill's.

Like her attitudes towards the natural world, the voice of Morag Gunn is in direct contrast to Hagar's, or Rachel's, or Stacey's voices. In the early novels Margaret Laurence was revealing the "ordinary" woman as extraordinary; here the writer, the "extraordinary" woman, one with a gift that forces her growth and her choices, is being modulated into the ordinary. Part of the author's intention is to capture as authentic a versimilitude to life as possible in the voice of Morag; an inseparable part of that intention is also to demonstrate the gap between Morag herself and the process of heightening that transpires as Morag "wrenches" a fictional character, Lilac Stonehouse, for instance, "out of her guts." Lilac, in the heightened, dramatized urgency of her voice, is more like Hagar, or Rachel, or Stacey, than is the voice of Morag. Those who miss a matching urgency in the voice of Morag have missed a major part of the intention of Margaret Laurence. We are given the dramatized, "fictionalized" Morag in the Memorybank Movies, but the voice of that Morag contrasts sharply, and is meant to contrast, to the woman of everyday life. The "real" Morag must deal moment by moment with her life and her problems; the luxury of self-dramatization is only permissible for her past self, or in her sporadic, humorous-confessional conversations with Catharine Traill.

In 1969 Margaret Laurence came back to Canada from

England to be writer-in-residence at Massey College, the University of Toronto. She had already decided that when her children's education was finished in England she must return to Canada. Shortly after she came to Toronto she bought a cabin on the Otonabee River near Peterborough. *The Diviners* was written over the next four years, partly in the winter-time in England, but mostly during the summers in Ontario. Its Ontario river-setting and the presence of Catharine Traill, a pioneer in the Peterborough area, are very obvious landmarks of Margaret Laurence's transition. But more than that, *The Diviners* is a homecoming novel, containing within it an epic of this land and its people, culminating and closing the Manawaka works with a quiet assurance that is Morag Gunn's affirmation—and Margaret Laurence's.

NINE

The Town—Our Tribe

Once it was the fashion to represent villages as
places inhabited by laughable, lovable sim-
pletons, unspotted by the worldliness of city
life, though occasionally shrewd in rural concerns. Later it was the popular thing to show
villages as rotten with vice, and especially such
sexual vice as Kraft-Ebing might have been
surprised to uncover in Vienna: incest, sodomy,
bestiality, sadism and masochism were supposed to rage behind lace curtains and in the
haylofts, while a rigid piety was professed in the
streets. Our village never seemed to me to be
like that. It was more varied in what it offered to
the observer than people from bigger and more
sophisticated places generally think, and if it had
sins and follies and roughnesses, it also had
much to show of virtue, dignity, and even of
nobility.

Robertson Davies, *Fifth Business*

Many Canadian writers have carried characters or settings
from one novel to another, among them Hugh MacLennan,
Mordecai Richler, Roch Carrier, and Mazo de la Roche. Many
others have used the small town as a setting—so many, in fact,
that a "Dictionary of Canadian Mythology" would contain a

very large entry under "Small Town." Elgin, Mariposa, Horizon, Deptford, Salterton, Crocus, and Jubilee would be major entries; besides Sara Jeannette Duncan, Stephen Leacock, Sinclair Ross, Robertson Davies, W. O. Mitchell, and Alice Munro, their authors, there would be many other names, contemporary authors like George Elliott, James Reaney, David Lewis, and Harry Boyle, or earlier ones like Adeline Teskey or Patrick Slater. But no town in our literature has been so consistently and extensively developed as Margaret Laurence's Manawaka. Through five works of fiction, it has grown as a vividly realized, microcosmic world, acting as a setting for the dilemmas of its unique individuals and also exercising its own powerful dynamic on them. Manawaka is also specifically, historically, and geographically authentic, dense with objects and true to its place and its development through time.

The towns of Canada were, in the beginning, our forts in the wilderness, not walled, armoured with guns, and policed by red-coated troops, but bulwarks all the same, civilization and supply centres for a raw, young country and the focal point for the dispensing of its trade. The earliest villages grew up around mill-sites where the settlers brought their grain to be ground, or around a travellers' crossroads where an inn and then a store had been built, or, in the West, along the railway lines. The towns developed from villages according to the demands made on them by the farmers around; a thriving town in 1880 meant a fertile agricultural land at its back. The towns grew according to various combinations of good land, good fortune—and the politics of railroad building. Their stars were in the ascendant during the last quarter of the nineteenth and the first two decades of the twentieth century, their brightest constellations beaded along the railway networks; after the First World War many of them gradually declined, reeling under the impact of the Depression of the thirties and drained of the young who got out when they could. Some towns are still backwaters of decline, some have become city suburbs and dormitories, and some, infused with life and direction by prosperity and new emigrants to Canada, have begun new cycles of change and growth. But historically, all of them are our community beginnings. Our literature is thick with their representations, memorials to their centrality in Canada's history and to the remarkable power of their effects, bad and good, upon our people.

The towns of Canadian literature provide us with illuminations of a major strand of our tradition, which is both historically and artistically true to our experience. For many Canadians a town was the matrix of social growth, the point of departure into a wider world and, inevitably for many, a point of no return. In the nineteenth and early twentieth centuries, writers such as Adeline Teskey in *Where the Sugar Maple Grows* and Patrick Slater in *The Yellow Briar* focused on the village or small town as a sentimentalized Utopia. Between 1900 and 1914 Sarah Jeannette Duncan in *The Imperialist* and Stephen Leacock in *Sunshine Sketches of a Little Town* recorded with their unique combinations of realism, affectionate irony, and satire the small Canadian town at the very peak of its corporate power and influence over its people. Later in the twenties, when, after the First World War, the dream of an innocent world was irrevocably lost, the satire became bitter and the details darker. In America, Sherwood Anderson's *Winesburg, Ohio* and Sinclair Lewis' *Mainstreet* were powerful patterns for small town portrayals, propelling writers towards revelations of individual loneliness and defeat, or satires on the hypocrisy, vulgarity, and general meanness of life in small closed communities. More recently, as Robertson Davies suggests, our writers from Reaney to Elliott to Margaret Laurence have given us portraits of the ambivalence of human experience within a small town.

But no writer has been in any doubt of one thing: the power and the influence of the town's corporate personality on its people, be they its heroes or its victims. The isolation of small groups of people in a vast land was one of the factors in the growth of a town's personality; in English Canada the other factor was the drive to build a progressive, successful, and Protestant community. Ideals of godliness and business enterprise were inextricably meshed and individuals were expected, both by commitment and from need, to adapt and to give evidence of their partnership in the community ideals by unremitting work, or to fall short of the corporate ideal at great personal loss and social peril. The town was our tribe—not, primarily, a network of kinship and family, but a powerful structure of hierarchical social relationships. The fact that everyone knew all about everyone else provided the framework of common knowledge, common interest, and gossip that held the town together. Talk, resented or enjoyed, malicious or concerned, both feared and welcomed, was the strong human communication-fabric of the town and was often stronger than the individual's communication lines through love or duty, trust, or even hate.

The community assigned roles to its people too; in the eyes of the town, individuals were often seen only in relation to their assigned roles. Generations of writers have realized that the town provides them with a setting that is both authentic and manageable, and also highly complex, highly dramatic, and ripe for explorations in the ironical distance between man as he seems to be and man as he really is. Christie Logan plays the part the town expects of him up to the hilt—and every town had its clowns—but the energy that brings Christie to life on the page lies in Margaret Laurence's successful fusing of his public and his private voices, clown and seer.

In Robertson Davies' *Fifth Business*, Dunstan Ramsay watches the towns people of Deptford burning the Kaiser in effigy to welcome their boys back from the First World War:

> And the people in the crowd, as I looked at them, were hardly recognizable as the earnest citizens who, not half an hour ago, had been so biddable under the spell of patriotic oratory, and so responsive to *Canadian born*. . . . Here they were, in this murky, fiery light, happily acquiescent in a symbolic act of cruelty and hatred . . . I watched them with dismay that mounted toward horror, for these were my own people.   (*Fifth Business*, p. 115)

"My own people" is the key to all the small-town literature. Narrow and constraining to the individual as the town may be, it was our kind of community, where everyone had his place—even the slot called "outsider" is better than no place at all—and where nobody's child could ever be lost.

Margaret Laurence's Manawaka world is Everyman's and Everywoman's, but its particularities are emphatically Canadian. Grounded in a small western town, her people move out into the wider world, but they carry Manawaka with them, its constraints and inhibitions, but also its sense of roots, of ancestors, and of a past that is living still, both its achievements and its tragic errors. A past so rooted, geographically and socially, is within the memory of many Canadians, and it is within the imaginative range of all.

The voices of Manawaka speak a Canadian vernacular, retained and recalled by Margaret Laurence and heightened according to the demands of her characters, but retaining its typical idioms and figures of speech, and particularly its irony of tone. A kind of self-mocking "survival humour" has always been associated with the Jewish voice and has been classically recorded for Canadians in Mordecai Richler's work; but the self-mocking voice of Hagar and the self-saving humour of Stacey are as truly authentic to Scotch-Irish Canadians, and Margaret Laurence's combination of ear and talent have recorded them.

Manawaka incorporates the general geographical and physical features of the town of Neepawa. Riding Mountain is Galloping Mountain, Clear Lake is Diamond Lake, and Manawaka's river is the Wachakwa. The town is not, strictly speaking, a prairie town, for it is still in the treed area: "Most of the country surrounding Neepawa was covered with scrub when the first settlers arrived. There were many poplar bluffs, and along the waterways there were heavier stands of timber" (*Neepawa, Land of Plenty*, p. 19). Manawaka has neither the flatness nor the unvegetated bleakness of Sinclair Ross' fictional Saskatchewan town of Horizon, for instance. The river, the hill on which the cemetery stands, the poplar bluffs, and the mountain in the distance provide major diversifications to its landscape, and its entire natural surroundings in their precise detail are often described in vignettes as beautiful, not ugly. The beauty is not blatant and does not force itself on the eye of the beholder, but it is everywhere present for the eye that can see it. Furthermore, Margaret Laurence often sets a natural beauty in contrast to a planned one; Hagar's memories of the scent of cowslips in the cemetery, the "tough-rooted . . . wild and gaudy flowers," stubbornly cancelling out the "funeral parlor perfume of the planted peonies," sets up and demonstrates the dichotomy between the works of man and nature that is basic to her description of Manawaka and to its deepest meaning.

Manawaka is the supply-centre for a farm region that is well cultivated and fruitful, except for the years of drought in the thirties. Even as it was described in *The Stone Angel* and *A Bird in the House*, the area was never completely barren:

> That part of the prairies where we lived was never dustbowl country. The farms around Manawaka never had a total crop failure, and afterwards, when the drought was over, people used to remark on this fact proudly. . . . But although Manawaka never knew the worst, what it knew was bad enough.
>
> (*A Bird in the House*, p. 136)

Galloping Mountain to the northwest symbolizes a kind of frontier of civilization and cultivation—and the possibility of freedom. It is there that Pique Tonnerre goes at the end of *The Diviners* to stay with her Uncle Jacques who has made a home for his own and all the other lost children of the Tonnerre family. Beyond the mountain is "up north," a land that belongs to another geography and seems as different as another country or another planet. This is the Shallow Creek country where Vanessa MacLeod visits her cousin Chris: "Shallow Creek seemed immeasurably far, part of a legendary winter country where no leaves grow and where the breath of seals and polar bears snuffled out steamily and turned to ice" (*A Bird in the House*, p. 128).

Manawaka's climate is one of extremes, the enervating heat of Rachel Cameron's summer holidays, or the blizzard in which a man might lose his life or lose, as Bram Shipley did, the horse that might have meant the fulfilment of his dreams. Ordinary weather is rarely described and almost never seen as being compatible to human comfort, though a mellow day can be used to point up the granite qualities of such a character as Grandfather Connor: "It was a warm day, the leaves turning a clear lemon yellow on the Manitoba maples and the late afternoon sun lighting up the windows of the Brick House like silver foil, but my grandfather was wearing his grey-heather sweater buttoned up to the neck" (*A Bird in the House*, p. 157).

Powerful though the town is in its effects on its people, Manawaka has no power over the cataclysmic events that batter them. The Depression and two wars simply and starkly happened *to* its people. Control is not in their hands, but as remote, as ominously and terrifying mysterious as the God of Wrath himself. People leave Manawaka and the land around it to go to "the west coast," to go to "the city," to go to the world wars, to go to the ladies' college in Ontario. Each of these destinations seems equally remote, as if on another planet. There is no idea or imagining, no warm encircling dream that joins Manawaka to any place outside, nor any important physical manifestation of joining in the way that the railway-networks are triumphant, almost magical, physical symbols of uniting far distances in the works of Thomas Wolfe and of Willa Cather.

In contrast, Manawaka's railroad runs *through* the town and west to Vancouver, the city that is the goal of hope and escape for many of the townspeople, and for some a place of final despair. Hagar went to Vancouver when she left Bram Shipley, and in a Vancouver hospital she finished her life. John Shipley faced himself in Vancouver in a way that his mother could not yet do, and he realized that his real place was in Manawaka with his father. Stacey Cameron couldn't wait to leave Manawaka for Vancouver, but at forty, trapped and desperate as she feels, Vancouver has become the very epitome of "The City Of The End Of Things" to her. To Rachel, Vancouver represents hope and a positive decision. She takes her mother and goes there to take her chances at living independent of the physical familiarity of Manawaka, at the same time recognizing that she carries the town always within her. Valentine Tonnerre, whom Stacey meets on the beach in *The Fire-Dwellers,* dies of drink and drugs on the streets of Vancouver. Thor Thorlakson, who in Manawaka was Vernon Winkler, beaten and bullied by his father, and Nick Kazlik's sister, Julie, are likewise refugees in Vancouver from Manawaka. Morag Gunn goes from Toronto to Vancouver to have her baby, to learn to accept her loneliness, and to support herself.

Throughout the works, Manawaka and Vancouver are polarized—Manawaka is "Town" as Vancouver is "City" and all the complications of rural and of urban life reside within the framework and the connotations of each respective place. To many Manawakans, Vancouver is escape and opportunity for life, but Stacey comes to see the place not only as a spiritual death-in-life but also as the site of imminent—and global—destruction. The drive of the men whom Hagar called "fledgling pharaohs in an uncouth land" has taken them right to the western rim of the continent and "The City" is their last, greatest, but most monstrous and inhuman monument.

After five books, the town of Manawaka can be specifically mapped. Its geography is precise and consistent, and there are now many landmarks in the town. At least two-score businesses and institutions have accumulated; some of them—Doherty's stables, Jarrett's bakery or the Queen Victoria Hotel—are simply reference points necessary to the setting, and others—Currie's General Store or Cameron's Funeral Home, later the Japonica Chapel—are essential focuses for the action of the various books. River Street runs south to the Wachakwa and north to the CPR tracks and Main Street intersects it. The Camerons live on Japonica Street, and Rachel, walking home from school, turns at River Street.

[I] walk past the quiet dark brick houses, too big for
their remaining occupants, built by somebody's
grandfathers who did well long ago out of a
brickworks or the first butcher shop. Long ago meaning half a century. Nothing is old here but it looks old.
The timber houses age fast, and even the brick looks
worn down after fifty years of blizzard winters and
blistering summers. They're put to shame by the new
bungalows like a bakery's pastel cakes, identical,
fresh, tasteless. This is known as a good part of town.
(*A Jest of God*, p. 10)

The cemetery, the garbage dump, and the valley where
the Tonnerres have their shacks are all on the outskirts of
Manawaka. The stone angel stands in the cemetery on a hill
overlooking the town. Christie Logan is garbage collector for
Manawaka and his "Nuisance Grounds" are not so very far
from the cemetery. This dump is the repository of the town's
rubbish, its discards and, sometimes, its awful secrets. In the
cemetery, death is set apart, kept within bounds in "the beauti-
fully cared-for habitations of the dead," as firmly and regularly
as rubbish is cast out and dug under in the "Nuisance
Grounds." Like death and garbage, the Métis family of
Tonnerres are outside the pale of Manawaka. The valley near
the dump where Pique Tonnerre burns to death with her
children is a place of horror for Morag Gunn, who was sent
there by Lachlan McLachlan to cover the story for the *Manawaka Banner*. But earlier, in her encounters with Jules
(Skinner) Tonnerre, the valley was also its own world apart, an
exotic place where Morag and Skinner explored making
friends and making love.

Out over the railway tracks is the trestle bridge where
John Shipley and Arlene Simmons died in a dare, and further
out from the town to the southwest is the Shipley farm. There
Bram Shipley dreamed of founding his dynasty and establishing his horse ranch, and there Hagar worked, loved, despaired
and dreamed of changing Bram into the mould of her father,
Jason Currie, a founder and pillar of Manawaka. About three

miles to the west of the town is the prosperous dairy farm of Nestor and Teresa Kazlik, Ukrainian immigrants whose past is almost lost to their children as Rachel Cameron's Scottish past is almost lost to her. Morag Gunn's parents, Colin and Louisa, also had a farm outside of Manawaka, but when they both died of polio in the thirties, the farm and all their other possessions had to go up for auction to pay off their mortgage.

When Hagar Currie was a child in the 1880's, Manawaka was still close to its beginnings, with board sidewalks, oil lamps, a few successful businesses such as Jason Currie's store, institutions such as the well-cared for cemetery, the ever-present undertakers and the churches, especially the Presbyterian church:

> I'd be about eight when the new Presbyterian church went up. Its opening service was the first time Father let me go to church with him instead of to Sunday School. It was plain and bare and smelled of paint and new wood, and they hadn't got the stained glass windows yet, but there were silver candlesticks at the front, each bearing a tiny plaque with Father's name, and he and several others had purchased family pews and furnished them with long cushions of brown and beige velour, so our few favoured bottoms would not be bothered by hard oak and a lengthy sermon.
>
> "On this great day," the Reverend Dougall MacCulloch said feelingly, "we have to give special thanks to those of our congregation whose generosity and Christian contributions have made our new church possible."
>
> He called them off, the names, like an honour role. Luke McVitie, lawyer. Jason Currie, businessman. Freeman McKendrick, bank manager. Burns MacIntosh, farmer. Rab Fraser, farmer.
>
> Father sat with modestly bowed head, but turned to me and whispered very low:

"I and Luke McVitie must've given the most, as he called our names the first."   (*The Stone Angel*, p. 15)

Not only Presbyterians came to towns like Manawaka. The Methodists, Baptists, Congregationalists, and all the other sects who established their churches in the small towns of Canada, carried with them religions that balanced far more towards fear than love. Certainly, everything men and women found in pioneer experience would confirm an impression that their God required hard service before rejoicing, as the land demanded battle from them and did not repay love. The God who presided over such a bleak experience must have seemed to the pioneers remarkably analogous to the Old Testament Jehovah, God of War and Wrath and Judgement.

Manawaka's was a swiftly forming social system, based on thrift, hard work, pressure to conform to the patterns of respectability, and, above all, financial success. In the beginning there were a few men, like the lawyer Luke McVitie and Jason Currie, who were "God-fearing," as Aunt Doll Stonehouse impressed upon Hagar, but who were even more emphatically "self-made." Jason Currie's pride impelled him to have Hagar educated in the faraway Ladies' College in Ontario and then to refuse to allow her to teach, insisting instead that she stay at home and be his lady-housekeeper. There were many other citizens of the town who saw and emulated such patterns, Lottie and Telford Simmons, for instance, who tried to wrap up their daughter Arlene in a cocoon of polite appearances and so lost her to John Shipley and death.

It was in the early days that the social map of the town was made with the "right" people and "the others" and, in geographical fact, a right and wrong side of the tracks. On the side farthest away from the railroad tracks there were a few big houses like the Currie's and many more modest, but eminently respectable ones. Near the tracks where land was cheap, or had been claimed simply by squatters' rights, were the houses and shacks of the poor, those who, like the Winklers, the Shinwells, and the Logans, were what the town called "shiftless" or simply unlucky. Three generations after its founding, in the twenties and thirties, when Stacey, Rachel, Vanessa, and Morag were children, the old standard in Man-awaka remained. Rachel and Stacey Cameron lived above the funeral parlor where their mother, desperate to keep up appearances, had become a harping hypochondriac, and Niall Cameron, their father, drank to forget that he lived more closely and more easily with death than with life. At the beginning of *A Bird in the House* Vanessa and her mother and father are living with Grandmother MacLeod whose house is among the few big houses of Manawaka. Grandmother mourns ceaselessly for the relatively luxurious and, by Manawaka's standards, even ostentatious way of life that vanished with the twenties:

> We had moved in with Grandmother MacLeod when the Depression got bad and she could no longer afford a housekeeper, but the MacLeod house never seemed like home to me. Its dark red brick was grown over at the front with Virginia creeper that turned crimson in the fall, until you could hardly tell brick from leaves. It boasted a small tower in which Grandmother MacLeod kept a weedy collection of anaemic ferns. The verandah was embellished with a profusion of wrought-iron scrolls, and the circular rose-window upstairs contained glass of many colours which permitted an outlooking eye to see the world as a place of absolute sapphire or emerald, or if one wished to look with a jaundiced eye, a hateful yellow. In Grandmother MacLeod's opinion, their features gave the house style.
>
> (*A Bird in the House,* p. 43)

After her father's death, Vanessa, her mother, and her brother have to go to live with Grandmother and Grandfather Connor. The yellow brick house, so solid, strong, and without ornament, but in itself so hard and plain, is a symbol of Grandfather's place as a "upright man" in the town, of his attitude to all those around him and to life itself:

That house in Manawaka is the one which, more than any other, I carry with me. Known to the rest of the town as "the old Connor place" and to the family as the Brick House, it was plain as the winter turnips in its root cellar, sparsely windowed as some crusader's embattled fortress in a heathen wilderness, its rooms in a perpetual gloom except in the brief height of summer. Many other brick structures had existed in Manawaka for as much as half a century, but at the time when my grandfather built his house, part dwelling place and part massive monument, it had been the first of its kind.

Set back at a decent distance from the street, it was screened by a line of spruce trees whose green-black branches swept down to the earth like the sternly protective wings of giant hawks. Spruce was not indigenous to that part of the prairies. Timothy Connor had brought the seedlings all the way from Galloping Mountain, a hundred miles north, not on whim, one may be sure, but feeling that they were the trees for him. By the mid-thirties, the spruces were taller than the house, and two generations of children had clutched at boughs which were as rough and hornily knuckled as the hands of old farmers, and had swung themselves up to the secret sanctuaries. On the lawn a few wild blue violets dared to grow, despite frequent beheadings from the clacking guillotine lawn mower, and mauve-flowered creeping Charley insinuated deceptively weak-looking tendrils up to the very edges of the flower beds where helmeted snapdragon stood in precision.

(A Bird in the House, p. 3)

The Manawaka works are dense with objects seen and described; this is particularly so of houses, which are shown as the shelters, the symbols—and the prisons—of those who live in them. Hagar, beleaguered by age and sickness, "can think of only one thing":

The house is mine. I bought it with the money I
worked for, in this city which has served as a kind of
home ever since I left the prairies. Perhaps it is not
home, as only the first of all can be truly that, but it is
mine and familiar. My shreds and remnants of years
are scattered through it visibly in lamps and vases,
the needle-point fire bench, the heavy oak chair from
the Shipley place, the china cabinet and walnut
sideboard from my father's house. There'd not be
room for all of these in some cramped apartment.
We'd have to put them into storage, or sell them. I
don't want that. I couldn't leave them. If I am not
somehow contained in them and in this house, something of all change caught and fixed here, eternal
enough for my purposes, then I do not know where I
am to be found at all.   (*The Stone Angel*, p. 36)

The language in which Vanessa recollects her
grandparents' houses directs our responses and sets up these
places as symbols of different, though equally constricting,
value systems. Mrs. MacLeod's house is "grown over with
virginia creepers"; it "boasted a small tower" with a "weedy
collection of ferns"; the verandah was "embellished" with a
"profusion" of wrought-iron scrolls, and out of the rose window
you could not see daylight, but "the world as a place of absolute
sapphire or emerald . . . or a hateful yellow." Grandmother
MacLeod lives in the world of the past and of her own
superficial illusions, and her house matches and reflects her.
On the other hand, Grandfather Connor's house was "plain as
the winter turnips in the root cellar," "sparsely windowed as
some crusader's embattled fortress," its rooms "in a perpetual
gloom except in the brief height of summer," and the whole,
"part dwelling place and part monument." The dualism of
Vanessa's years with her grandfather and of her feeling for him
is established in her description of the spruces outside, whose
branches swept down to earth "like the sternly protective
wings of giant hawks." Here, as in the description of the
cemetery in the first pages of *The Stone Angel*, Margaret

Laurence sets up the dichotomy between what man undertakes to order and civilize and the marginal but insistent freedom of the works of nature: The planted snapdragons are "helmeted" and they "stand in precision," but violets dare to grow on the lawn despite the "guillotine" lawnmower. And the creeping Charlie moves "its deceptively weak-looking tendrils" right up to the edges of the ordered flower beds.

There are five major and interacting family connections in Manawaka and these now stretch over four generations: the Curries and the Shipleys; the Camerons and the Kazliks; the Connors and the MacLeods; the Gunns and the Logans; and the Tonnerres. Many others—Henry Pearl and Luke McVitie, Doctor Cates and Lachlan McLachlan, Lottie Simmons and Eva and Vernon Winkler among them—come in and out of two or more of the works with brief but vivid impacts. Manawaka's timespan comes up from the early 1880's, the childhood of Hagar, to the present; Pique Tonnerre is four generations on from her great-grandfather, Jules Tonnerre, as Stephen Shipley, Hagar's grandson, is from Jason Currie. In *The Diviners*, however, it is made clear that the townspeople incorporate in their bones and blood a far longer span of history than the town's, one that comes down from the time of the Highland Clearances and from before the settlement of the West, and is landmarked by battles—Batoche, Bourlon Wood, and Dieppe.

Manawaka is a fully realized, three-dimensional, imagined town of length, breadth, and depth, and of history and corporate personality. We can orient ourselves to its social structure, as to its streets and buildings. Through the stories of its people, we can make connection with the present and the past of the people of Canada, their aspirations and failures—and our own. Manawaka also possesses, implies, and constantly reveals beneath its surfaces the fourth dimension of time and the timeless, of men and women as the victims and prisoners of the institutions they have made for their own survival, and of the endless, stumbling pilgrimage of the Tribe of Man towards God.

TEN

And That One Talent

"Her secret? It is every artist's secret"—he waved his hand—"passion. That is all. It is an open secret, and perfectly safe. Like heroism, it is inimitable in cheap materials."

Willa Cather, *Song of the Lark*

Margaret Laurence is a writer by destiny—and then by hard choice and long training. Her life and her work are inseparable and they are as much the fulfilling of early prophecy as Morag Gunn's, though there is nothing as strange in Morag's development as the role played by chance in the consolidating of Margaret Laurence's talent. Her urge to write was, from childhood, very strong, but so were the inhibitions of her time and place: "For many years I did not believe that writing could be one's profession." The chances that sent the Laurences to Africa in 1952 provided the great catalyst in the releasing and uninhibiting of her talent. Her experiences of Africa issued in works that explored themes of exile, loss, and mankind's stubborn, valiant quests for home and freedom; they also led her to see that these themes were particularly urgent to her own people as well. For culturally, Canada is also an emergent nation. The colonial temper of mind is hard to vanquish and we have been doubly vulnerable to borrowed cultures, both Britain's and America's. We are still anxious

and tentative about defining ourselves by this land and this
land only, and as much as Africans, or West Indians, we need
our writers to show us who we are and where we stand.

Margaret Laurence found her common ground and common purpose among the writers of the emergent nations, the
Nigerians, Chinua Achebe and Wole Soyinka in particular, but
also West Indians such as Edward Brathwaite, Derek Walcott,
and George Lamming. She shares with them a commitment so
strong that it is really a sense of mission, to explore and
illuminate the past of their peoples in order to bring a sense of
dignity and continuity to the lives of men and women in the
present. An "act of restitution," Gerald Moore calls it, speaking of the work of Achebe, "necessary both as a piece of social
history and as offering a ground for some sort of cultural
continuity" (Gerald Moore, *The Chosen Tongue*, p. 151).

In 1966 Margaret Laurence began a study of Nigerian
dramatists and novelists from 1952 to 1966. The book, *Long
Drums and Cannons*, published by Macmillan of England in
1968, is a work of expository scholarship and careful background research into tribal rites and customs. Lines from
Christopher Okigbo's *Heavensgate* are its epigraph:

> I have visited the prodigal . . .
> in palmgrove,
> long-drums and cannons:
> the spirit in the ascent.

"The spirit in the ascent" is also the core and the containing
theme of all Margaret Laurence's work, and in its totality,
Long Drums and Cannons is both a tribute to her particular
"tribe" among all the writers of the world and, in certain areas,
a statement that clarifies the purpose she holds in common
with them. In her preface she stresses the importance of the
attempts made by these Nigerian novelists to interpret Africa
from the inside and to restore the value of the past "without
idealising it and without being shackled by it." At the same
time, no writer can allow himself to be disengaged from the
events and problems of his own time:

> The clash between generations, the several and in-
> dividual disturbances brought about by a period of
> transition, the slow dying of the destructive aspects
> of tribalism, the anguish and inadequacy of uncom-
> promising individualism as an alternative to
> tribalism.   (*Long Drums and Cannons*, Preface)

Her final statement broadens out to become a manifesto for the
work of all writers everywhere:

> Perhaps the most enduringly interesting aspect of
> Nigerian literature, however, as of literature every-
> where, is the insight it gives not only into immediate
> and local dilemmas but, through these, into the
> human dilemma as a whole. Literature can only do
> this in very specific and detailed ways. It must be
> planted firmly in some soil. Even works of non-
> realism make use of spiritual landscapes which have
> been at least partially inherited by the writer.
> Despite some current fashions to the contrary, the
> main concern of a writer remains that of somehow
> creating the individual on the printed page, of catch-
> ing the tones and accents of human speech, of setting
> down the conflicts of people who are as real to him as
> himself. If he does this well, and as truthfully as he
> can, his writing may sometimes reach out beyond any
> national boundary.
>   (*Long Drums and Cannons,* Preface)

In "catching the tones and accents of human speech,"
Achebe of Nigeria has transferred the Ibo language, its tales
and proverbs, and particularly its great wealth of nature-
imagery, into English prose of great artistry. The strength and
impact of Margaret Laurence's work lies as surely in her
language as does Achebe's. She, too, has listened to her people, and in a very real artist's sense she has "made" their
language and transferred it to paper. Its sounds, its idioms, and
its images are authentic to our speech and our experience, but

the richness of its texture and its interweaving and recurring image-patterns are Margaret Laurence's achievement and hers alone.

In *The Diviners*, Margaret Laurence showed us the two developing, interflowing streams of Morag Gunn's birth and growth as a writer—the truthfulness of vision and the unremitting effort to create the individual on the printed page. In *Long Drums and Cannons*, she writes of Chinua Achebe's constant concern with "human communication and the lack of it," in words which also apply to all her own works:

> He shows the impossibly complicated difficulties of one person speaking to another, attempting to make himself known to another, attempting to hear—really to hear—what another is saying. In his novels, we see man as a creature whose means of communication are both infinitely subtle and infinitely clumsy, a prey to invariable misunderstandings. Yet Achebe's writing also conveys the feeling that we must attempt to communicate, however imperfectly, if we are not to succumb to despair or madness. The words which are spoken are rarely the words which are heard, but we must go on speaking.
>
> (*Long Drums and Cannons*, p. 124)

Chinua Achebe himself has written his manifesto of the writer's purpose in words that also define Margaret Laurence's purpose in all her works.

> The worst thing that can happen to any people is the loss of their dignity and self-respect. The writer's duty is to help them regain it by showing them in human terms what happened to them, what they lost. There is a saying in Ibo that a man who can't tell where the rain began to beat him cannot know where he dried his body. The writer can tell the people where the rain began to beat them. After all the writer's duty is not to beat this morning's headline in

topicality, it is to explore in depth the human condition. In Africa he cannot perform this task unless he
has a proper sense of history.   ("The Role of a Writer
   in a New Nation," *Nigeria Magazine*, 81 (1964)

Margaret Laurence has been painfully aware of the failures in
dignity and self-respect among all men and women and
particularly among her own people.

From "Drummer of All the World" to *The Diviners*, she
has created characters who achieve immediate communication
with us. They bear witness to our own aspirations and
tragedies; their laughter confirms both joy and endurance; and
above all, their energy affirms man's astonishing power to
grow. Among them, the five women, Hagar, Rachel, Stacey,
Vanessa and Morag, are pre-eminent. These characters did not
happen because Margaret Laurence set herself a special goal of
writing novels about women, and certainly not because she has
not been successful with male characters (Archipelago, Johnny
Kestoe, Bram Shipley, Grandfather Connor, Jules Tonnerre
and Christie Logan are a creditable gallery!). They came to
being out of the depth of her early experience in a small
Manitoba town. They grew through her adult perceptions
about how it was—and is—to be an individual woman in a
specific Canadian time and place. And in the broadest and
deepest ways, their strengths and their vulnerabilities make
connections with all women, everywhere.

Women readers of the Manawaka works feel a special
gratitude for Hagar, Rachel, Stacey, Morag, and Vanessa, and
Canadian women a special identification with them. As
Margaret Laurence has often said, in America Hagar was con-
sidered the archetypal North American old woman; in Canada
she was everybody's grandmother. Out of the Manawaka
background, common to many of us and within the imaginative
range of all of us, in a timespan of almost a century, each of
these women is battered by events, but also moves of her own
free will towards self-recognition, self-acceptance, and the
awareness of a limited freedom. They are all intensely and
introspectively aware of themselves, but the demons of self-

dramatization, self-pity, and sentimentality do not obscure their vision or block their progress. They endure and they grow, gradually shaking off debilitating guilts and fears and learning to accept themselves as well as others with tolerance and love. That same journey is, of course, the necessary primary foundation of any individual's liberation.

These women do not come through as larger-than-life, mythic figures or as tragic heroines, elevated and distanced from our ordinary experience. Stacey's final words in *The Fire-Dwellers*, "Give me another forty years Lord, and I may mutate into a matriarch," rings its note of humourous irony back over the whole work. She has indeed *been* a matriarch in her desire to hold and protect her children exclusive of Mac and all the world around her. What she has done, in the course of the weeks of her ordeal, is to mutate into a human being with a certain confidence in her own individuality and an equal acceptance of her limitations and of life's.

All of Margaret Laurence's women are strong and strongly maternal. They also feel the imperatives of emotion, of guilt and desire, sexuality and individuality that all women share. And they live, as we do, among the tensions set up between their individual, inner needs and the demands that society imposes on them from the outside. They achieve only the precarious balance that might conceivably issue from their temperaments and their situations. But they do issue as individuals and as members of the human race, with dignity and potential, rights and responsibilities, which are insistently shown to be equal to men's. Margaret Laurence's great gift to us is that they come indomitably through the pages, with laughter, with bravery, and with reassurance—our ancestors, our sisters, and our friends.

Bibliographic Checklist

Books by Margaret Laurence

A Tree for Poverty; Somali Poetry and Prose. Published for the British Protectorate of Somaliland. Nairobi: Eagle Press, 1954. Reprint Dublin: Irish University Press, 1970, Hamilton: McMaster University, 1970.

This Side Jordan. Toronto: McClelland and Stewart, London: Macmillan, New York: St. Martin's Press, 1960.

The Tomorrow-Tamer. Toronto: McClelland and Stewart, London: Macmillan, 1963, New York: Knopf, 1964.

Die Stimmen von Adamo. Translation of *The Tomorrow-Tamer.* Munich; Zurich: Droemer Knaur, 1965.

The Tomorrow-Tamer and Other Stories. Introduction by Clara Thomas. N.C.L. Toronto: McClelland and Stewart, 1970.

The Prophet's Camel Bell. Toronto: McClelland and Stewart, London: Macmillan, 1963. Published under the title *New Wind in a Dry Land.* New York: Knopf, 1964.

The Stone Angel. Toronto: McClelland and Stewart, London: Macmillan, New York: Knopf, 1964.

Der Steinerne Engel. Translation of *The Stone Angel.* Munich; Zurich: Droemer Knaur, 1965.

The Stone Angel. Introduction by William H. New. N.C.L. Toronto: McClelland and Stewart, 1968.

A Jest of God. Toronto: McClelland and Stewart, London: Macmillan, New York: Knopf, 1966.

Long Drums and Cannons: Nigerian Dramatists and Novelists 1952-1966. London: Macmillan, 1968. New York: Praeger, 1969.

Raquel, Raquel. Translation of *A Jest of God* by Agustin Gil Lasierra. Barcelona: Ediciones Grijalbo, 1969.

A Jest of God. Introduction by G. D. Killam. N.C.L. Toronto: McClelland and Stewart, 1974.

The Fire-Dwellers. Toronto: McClelland and Stewart, London: Macmillan, New York: Knopf, 1969. *The Fire-Dwellers.* St. Albans, Herts: Panther Books, 1973.

The Fire-Dwellers. Introduction by Allan Bevan. N.C.L. Toronto: McClelland and Stewart, 1973.

Ta Maison est en Feu. Translation of *The Fire-Dwellers* by Rosine Fitzgerald. Paris: Editions Stock, Montreal: H.M.H., 1971.

A Bird in the House; Stories. Toronto: McClelland and Stewart, New York: Knopf, London: Macmillan, 1970.

A Bird in the House. Introduction by Robert Gibbs. N.C.L. Toronto: McClelland and Stewart, 1974.

Jason's Quest. Illustrated by Staffan Torell. Toronto: McClelland and Stewart, New York: Knopf, London: Macmillan, 1970.

The Diviners. Toronto: McClelland and Stewart, New York: Knopf, London: Macmillan, 1974.

Works about Margaret Laurence

The following checklist of papers, held at the Scott Library, York University, was compiled by Margaret Pappert.

Articles

Asante, N. "Margaret (Rachel, Rachel) Laurence." *Montrealer* 43 (June 1969): 30-3.

Atwood, Margaret. "Face to Face." *Maclean's Magazine* 87 (May 1974): 38-9;43-6.

Barling, Ann. "Interview with Laurence." *Vancouver Sun*, September 24, 1966.

Bowering, G. "That fool of a fear: notes on 'A Jest of God'." *Canadian Literature* 50 (Autumn 1971): 41-56.

Callaghan, B. "Writings of Margaret Laurence." *Tamarack Review* 36 (Summer 1965): 45-51.

Currer, Lete. "Margaret Laurence: The Tomorrow Tamer and This Side Jordan." Typewritten essay.

Djwa, Sandra. "False Gods and the True Covenant: Thematic Continuity Between Margaret Laurence and Sinclair Ross." *Journal of Canadian Fiction* 1 (Fall 1972): 4, 43-50.

Engel, Marion. "Margaret Laurence." *Chatelaine* 47 (May 1974): 25.

French, William. "Margaret Laurence: Her Books Rear Up and Demand To Be Written." *Globe and Mail*, April 25, 1970.

Fulford, Robert. "Margaret Laurence Come To Town." *Toronto Daily Star*, August 10, 1966.

Hinds, Barbara. "Distinguished Canadian Writer, Her First Editor, Have Reunion." *Halifax Mail Star*, March 12, 1970.

Kreisel, H. "Familiar Landscape." *The Tamarack Review* 55: 91-2.

Legate, David M. Review of *Margaret Laurence* by Clara Thomas. *Montreal Star*, May 3, 1969.

Legge, Helen K. "W.I. Woman is provincial title-winner." *Pointe Claire Lakeshore News and Chronicle*, Quebec, August 1, 1974.

McCracken, Melinda. Interview. *Winnipeg Free Press*, February 27, 1964.

McLay, C.M. "Every man is an island: isolation in 'A Jest of God'." *Canadian Literature* 50 (Autumn 1971): 57-68.

Martin, Ruth. Interview. *Smith's Trade News* (London), February 29, 1964.

Palmateer, D.A. "Irony In The Short Stories of Margaret Laurence and The Novels of Chinua Achebe." Typewritten essay.

Parameswaran, Forman, Denyse and Uma. "Echoes and Refrains in the Canadian Novels of Margaret Laurence." *The Centennial Review* 16: 233-53.

Pesando, Frank. "In a Nameless Land: The Use of Apocalyptic Mythology in the Writings of Margaret Laurence." *Journal of Canadian Fiction* 2 (Winter 1973): 1, 53-57.

Read, S.E. Essay on Laurence's literary career. Rough typed draft. No date.

Read, S.E. "The Maze of Life: The Work of Margaret Laurence." *Canadian Literature* 27: 5-14.

Saunders, Tom. Interview with Laurence. *Winnipeg Free Press*, October 7, 1966.

Saunders, Tom. Article on Laurence. "Writers and Books." *Winnipeg Free Press*, September 30, 1966.

Silver, David. "The Theme of Journey and Return In the Works of Margaret Laurence." Typewritten essay.

Stainsby, Donald. Letter defending Prism and praising "The Merchant of Heaven." *Vancouver Sun*, no date.

Thomas, Clara. "Proud Lineage: Willa Cather and Margaret Laurence." Typewritten essay.

Thomas, Clara. "Proud Lineage." Willa Cather and Margaret Laurence," *Canadian Review of American Studies* 2 (Spring 1971): 1, 3-12.

Thomas, Clara. "The Novels of Margaret Laurence." *Studies in the Novel*, University of Texas, 4 (Summer 1972): 2, 154-164.

Thomas, Clara. "The Short Stories of Margaret Laurence." *World Literature Written In English*. 11, i: 25-33.

Thomas, Clara, transcriber. "A Conversation about Literature: An Interview with Margaret Laurence and Irving Layton." *Journal of Canadian Fiction* 1, i: 65-69.

Wigmore, D. "Margaret Laurence: the woman behind the writing." *Chatelaine* 44 (Fall 1971): 28-9.

Wilkens, Emily. Announcement of Laurence's appointment as writer-in-residence at the University of Toronto. *Barrie Examiner*, February 25, 1970.

Wilson, Ethel. Letter praising Laurence's "The Merchant of Heaven." *Prism*, Winter 1959.

"Revolutionary Ad." *Evening Standard*, July 3, 1969.

"His Job is Bad Entertainer." *Cornwall Standard Freeholder*, August 5, 1970.

Interview with Laurence. *Books and Bookmen*. No date. pp. 26-28.

"Laurence of Manitoba." *Canadian Authors and Bookmen* 42 (Winter 1966): 4-7.

"Portrait." *Maclean's Magazine* 79 (January 1966): 55.

"Portrait." *Canadian Authors and Bookmen* 39 (Spring 1964): cover.

[President's medal, University of Western Ontario awarded to Margaret Laurence.] *Tamarack Review* 32 (Summer 1964): 103.

Portrait. *Chatelaine* 42 (June 1969): 8

Portrait. *Saturday Night* 84 (May 1969): 38.

Reviews

The Prophet's Camel Bell

Girling, H.K. Review of *The Prophet's Camel Bell. Queen's Quarterly* 71 (Autumn 1964): 456-7.

Holloway, David. "Travels and Misadventures." *Telegraph.* No date.

Prescott, Orville. "Life With the Nomads of Somaliland." *New York Times,* June 17, 1964.

S.N. Review of *The Prophet's Camel Bell. Books and Bookmen,* October 1963.

Stewart, Desmond. Review of *The Prophet's Camel Bell. The Arab Observer* (Cairo). Typewritten draft.

Watmough, David. Script of radio review of *The Prophet's Camel Bell.* CBC Radio, Vancouver, October 11, 1963.

Wordsworth, Christopher. "Review of The Prophet's Camel Bell." *The Guardian* (Manchester, England), September 20, 1963.

"On the Colonial Heritage: the whites aren't *all* blackhearted." *Maclean's Reviews* 76 (October 19, 1963): 20.

"Job Worth Doing." *Oxford Mail* (Oxford, England), August 15, 1963.

Review of *The Prophet's Camel Bell. Canadian Fiction* 43 (Fall 1964): 259.

Review of *The Prophet's Camel Bell. Saturday Night* 79 (January 1964): 25-6.

Review of *The Prophet's Camel Bell. Tamarack Review* 31 (Spring 1964): 98.

Review of *The Prophet's Camel Bell. University of Toronto Quarterly* 33 (July 1964): 431-2.

New Wind in a Dry Land

Magid, Nora. Review of *New Wind In A Dry Land. The Reporter,* July 2, 1964.

Miller, Charles. Review of *New Wind in a Dry Land. Saturday Review,* June 13, 1964.

This Side Jordan

Kreisel, Henry. "The African Stories of Margaret Laurence." *The Canadian Forum,* April 1961.

Review of *This Side Jordan. British Columbia Library Quarterly* 25 (July 1961): 31, 34.

Review of *This Side Jordan. Canadian Comment* 5 (Fall 1961): 13-14.

Review of *This Side Jordan. Canadian Literature* 8 (Spring 1961): 62-3.

Review of *This Side Jordan. University of Toronto Quarterly* 30 (July 1961): 406-7.

Triumvirate: The Stone Angel, New Wind in a Dry Land, The Tomorrow-Tamer.

Barkham, John. "Three Arrows From One Bow." *Saturday Review Syndicate.* Draft.

Fuller, Edmund. "Diversity in Triplicate." *Chicago Tribune,* June 14, 1964.

Leclair, Edward E. "Author's Varied Talents Proven by Three Works." *Sunday Times—Union* (Albany, N.Y.), June 21, 1964.

Pickael, Paul. "Triple Debut." *Harpers*, July, 1964.

"Three At Once by One Author." *Detroit News*, June 21, 1964.

The Tomorrow-Tamer

Anderson, Doris. *The Tomorrow-Tamer and Other Stories. Canadian Reader*, March 1964, pp. 2-3.

Bishop, Dorothy. Review of *The Tomorrow-Tamer, Ottawa Journal*, January 25, 1964.

B.P. "Versatile Canadian," *Montreal Star*, February 22, 1964.

Bryson, Artemisia B. "Book Captures Africa's Tragedy, Fetishes," *Fort Worth Telegram*, August 2, 1964.

Campbell, Michael. Review of *The Tomorrow-Tamer*. No title or date.

French, William. "Colourful Tales of Modern Africa." *Globe and Mail* (Toronto), February 1, 1964.

Granthan, Ronald. "Private Dramas Created As West Africa Changes." *Ottawa Citizen*, February 3, 1964.

Kirkwood, Hilda. "The Compassionate Eye." *The Canadian Forum* 44 (July, 1964): 94.

Leslie, Andrew. Review of *The Tomorrow-Tamer. The Guardian* (Manchester), October 18, 1963.

McKenna, Isobel. "Something Old—Something New." *The Guardian* (Manchester), July 23, 1970.

McNay, M.G. Review of *The Tomorrow-Tamer. Oxford Mail*, October 3, 1963.

M.L.H. "A thrilling group of African Tales." *The Winnipeg Tribune*, February 1, 1964.

Parfet, Ione. "Short Stories Reflect Africa's Beauty and Racial Problems." *Wichita Falls Times*, June 14, 1964.

Parton, Lorne. Review of *The Tomorrow-Tamer, Vancouver Province*, February 1, 1964.

Robson, John. Review of *The Tomorrow-Tamer. Toronto Telegram*, February 11, 1964.

Saunders, Tom. "Caught in The Winds of Change." *Winnipeg Free Press*, January 25, 1964.

Tahir, Ibrahim. "Anthropological Curiosity?" *West Africa*, (London), November 9, 1963.

"African Crosscurrents." *The Times Literary Supplement* (London), October 25, 1963.

Review of *The Tomorrow-Tamer* and *New Wind in a Dry Land. The Atlantic Monthly*, September 1964.

Weaver, Robert. "Margaret Laurence Sets Mad Publishing Pace." Newspaper, no date.

Review of *The Tomorrow-Tamer. Canadian Literature* 45 (Summer 1970): 82-4.

Review of *The Tomorrow-Tamer. University of Toronto Quarterly* 34 (July 1965): 375-6.

Review of *The Tomorrow-Tamer. Canadian Authors and Bookmen* 39 (Spring 1964): 10.

Review of *The Tomorrow-Tamer. Canadian Literature* 21 (Summer 1964): 53-5.

Review of *The Tomorrow-Tamer. Montrealer* 38 (May 1964): 37-8.
Review of *The Tomorrow-Tamer. Tamarack Review* 31 (Spring 1964): 92-3.

The Stone Angel

Bennette, Joan. Review of *The Stone Angel. Glasgow Herald*, March 7, 1964.

Coulthard, Elizabeth. Review of *The Stone Angel. The Observer*, October 1, 1964.

Davies, Robertson. "Self-Imprisoned to Keep the World at Bay." *New York Times Book Review*, June 14, 1964.

DeProse, Molly. "A book for nearly everyone." *Ottawa Citizen*, 1964.

D.M.L. "A Strindberg Figure." *Montreal Star*, May 23, 1964.

Fane, Vernon. Brief mention of *The Stone Angel. Sphere* (London), March 21, 1964.

Graham, Kathleen. Review of *The Stone Angel. The Leader-Post* (Regina), June 6, 1964.

Hicks, Granville. "Neighbor to the North Makes News." *Saturday Review*, June 13, 1964, pp. 25-26.

Hodgson, Rose Marie. "Grow Old Along With Me." *Bridlington Free Press* (Yorkshire), April 24, 1964.

G.T. "Coming To Terms With Time." *Oldham Evening Chronicle and Standard* (Lancashire), March 16, 1964.

H.T.K. "A Bleak Soul." *The Canadian Forum* 44 (August, 1964): 117.

Jackel, Susan. "Rage, rage ..." *Summer Varsity*, August 14, 1964.

J.S. "Involving the Reader In a Special World." *Saskatoon-Star Phoenix*, August 23, 1964.

Kattan, Naim. "L'Ouest canadien sans voiles." *Le Devoir*, August 29, 1964.

Kervin, Roy. "Rich Reading About Canada." *The Gazette*, August 30, 1964.

Meynell, Laurence. Review of *The Stone Angel. Express and Star* (Wolverhampton, Staffordshire), March 6, 1964.

M.L.H. "Manitoba Setting for native-born Writer's new tale." *Winnipeg Tribune*, May 23, 1964.

Moir, Nikki. "Descriptions of people and places pure poetry." *The Province*, May 30, 1964.

Montagnes, Anne. "Piercing Canadian Symbol." Book Review Section, *The Globe and Mail*. June 13, 1964, p. 17.

O'Brien, E.D. Review of *The Stone Angel, Illustrated London News*, April 18, 1964.

Oliver, Mark. "Pathos of Longevity," *Eastern Daily Press* (Norwich, Norfolk), March 6, 1964.

Pick L. Rough draft of a review of *The Stone Angel*, and two letters from the author to Laurence concerning the writing of the review for Book Review Class of N.Y. School of Social Research. September 13, 1965 and July 4, 1965.

P.W.L. "Canadian Writes Perceptive Novel of Prairie Life and Old Age." *The Albertan*, September 5, 1964.

P.T.H. Review of *The Stone Angel. Sunday Independent* (Dublin), March 8, 1964.

Robson, John. Review of *The Stone Angel. The Telegram* (Toronto), May 29, 1964.

Saunders, Tom. "A Novel of Competence." *Winnipeg Free Press,* May 23, 1964.

Saunders, Tom. Review of *The Stone Angel. University of Manitoba Alumni Journal.*

Stainsby, Donald. Review of *The Stone Angel. Victoria Daily Times,* May 23, 1964.

Tracy, Honor. "A Writer of Major Talent." *New Republic,* June 20, 1964.

Weaver, Robert. "Crowning 'Angel'." *The Daily Star* (Toronto), May 23, 1964.

Whately, Rosaleen. Review of *The Stone Angel. Liverpool Daily Post,* March 11, 1964.

Review of *The Stone Angel. Time,* July 24, 1964, p. 68.

Review of *The Stone Angel. Alphabet* 10 (July 1965): 85-6.

Review of *The Stone Angel. British Columbia Library Quarterly* 28 (July-October 1964): 41, 43-4.

Review of *The Stone Angel. Tamarack Review* 33 (Autumn 1964): 92-4.

Review of *The Stone Angel. University of Toronto Quarterly* 34 (July 1965): 373-5.

Review of *The Stone Angel. Canadian Authors and Bookmen* 40 (Autumn 1964): 17.

Review of *The Stone Angel. Canadian Literature* 21 (Summer 1964): 53-5.

Review of *The Stone Angel. Pictou Advocate* (Nova Scotia), May 29, 1974.

"*Stone Angel* Theme Symbolism of Water." *Sault St. Marie Star,* May 10, 1974.

A Jest of God

Baird, Dorwin and Verna. Radio review of *A Jest of God.* Book Mark Radio Series, 19 B.C. and Yukon Radio Stations, October 1966.

Ball, David. Review of *A Jest of God. The Tribune* (London), August 26, 1966.

Bannerman. "The Passion of a Prairie Spinster." *Maclean's Reviews,* October 1, 1966.

Bennett, Alice K. "Lonely Teacher's Bittersweet Idyll." *The Dallas Morning News,* August 28, 1966.

Bishop, Dorothy. Review of *A Jest of God. Ottawa Journal,* September 17, 1966.

Bowen, Ruth. "Talk About 'Rachel'." *Edmonton Journal,* October 4, 1966.

Bresler, Riva T. Review of *A Jest of God. Library Journal* (New York), August 1966.

Cameron, Donald. Review of *A Jest of God. Journal of Commonwealth Literature* 5 (1968): 133-5.

Clapperton, Jane. "A Girl Who Pulls Doors Marked 'Push'." *Life Book Review,* September 24, 1966.

Cooper, William. Review of *A Jest of God. The Listener,* August 25, 1966.

Daniel, John. Review of *A Jest of God. Spectator,* July 8, 1966.

Denton, Helen. Review of *A Jest of God. Prince George Progress,* October 19, 1966.

DeProse, Molly. "Prairie Pattern Depicted But Teacher is Baffling". *Ottawa Citizen,* November 12, 1966.

D.M.L. "Margaret Laurence's Brilliant Study." *The Montreal Star,*
September 10, 1966.

Donnelly, Terry. Review of *A Jest of God. The Gateway* (Edmonton),
November 10, 1966.

French, Doris. Radio Review of *A Jest of God. Morning Commentary,*
September 15, 1966.

Fulford, Robert. "A painful life in a prairie town." *The Daily Star*
(Toronto), September 30, 1966.

Gordon, Michael. Review of *A Jest of God.* C.B.C. National Network,
September 27, 1966.

Grosskurth, Phyllis. "Pathos Not Quite Enough." Book Review Section,
Globe and Mail.

Hall, Joan Joffe. "Prison of the Self." *Saturday Review,* August 27, 1966.

Hancox, Ralph. "God's jokes with men and man's with God." *Peterborough
Examiner,* October 8, 1966.

Jeffery, Mildred. Review of *A Jest of God. New Westminister Columbian*
(B.C.), October 7, 1966.

J.K.E. "Writes of Hometown." October 8, 1966.

Obodiac, Stan. "Reviewing 'A Jest of God'." *Toronto Danforth Tribune,*
September 29, 1966.

J.P. "Remarkable Book By Fine Writer." *Calgary Herald,* November 18,
1966.

J.S. "Irony Used to Magnificent Advantage." *Saskatoon Star Phoenix,*
September 17, 1966.

Read, S.E. Review of *A Jest of God. Book Reviews,* no date pp. 23-25.

Ready, William. Review of *A Jest of God. Hamilton Spectator,* September
17, 1966.

Rose, Jeanne. "Struggle for a fuller life." *Baltimore Sunday Sun,* September
4, 1966.

Rosengarten, H.J. "Inescapable Bonds." *Canadian Literature* (Winter
1968): 99-100.

Sheppard, R.Z. "Love's Labour's Lost." *Chicago Sun-Times,* September 25,
1966.

Simon, Marion, "Unusual Insight In the Touching 'A Jest of God'." *The
National Observer,* August 29, 1966.

St. George Stubbs, Roy. "The Laurence Magic Slumbers" *Winnipeg Free
Press,* September 24, 1966.

T.A.J. "Small Town Teacher." *Lethbridge Herald* (Alberta), December 10,
1966.

Thornton, Eugenia. "An Honourable Piece of Fiction." *The Plain Dealer*
(Cleveland), September 11, 1966.

Urquahar, Fred. "Trapped in a Prairie Town." *Oxford Mail* (England), no
date.

Review of *A Jest of God. Daily Journal Record* (Oakville Ont.), October 5,
1966.

Review of *A Jest of God. Atlantic Advocate* 57 (May 1967): 78.

Review of *A Jest of God. British Columbia Library Quarterly* 30 (October
1966): 23-5.

Review of *A Jest of God. Canadian Literature* 31 (Winter 1967): 71-2, 74-5.

Review of *A Jest of God. Tamarack Review* 42 (Winter 1967): 80-2.
Review of *A Jest of God. University of Toronto Quarterly* 36 (July 1967):
382.
Review of *A Jest of God. Leamington Post and News*, September 4, 1974.

Long Drums and Cannons

Beeching, D.H. "They Came to Know This 'Fierce Land'." *Victoria Daily
Times*, January 18, 1964.
Lancour, Harold. Advance review of *Long Drums and Cannons. Library
Journal*, March 15, 1969.
Nkosi, Lewis. "Who are the Africans?" *The Guardian* (London), January 3,
1969.
Nkosi, Lewis. "A Question of Literary Stewardship." *Africa Report*,
May-June 1969, pp. 69-71.
Piquefort. "Long Drums and Cannons and Ilyushins." *The Canadian Forum*
48 (Fall 1969): 249.
"Ways Into Africa." *Times Literary Supplement* (London), January 2, 1969.
Review of *Long Drums and Cannons. Negro Digest*, February 1970.
A review of *Long Drums and Cannons* and W. Cartey's *Whispers From a
Continent:* The Literature of Contemporary Black Africa. Typewritten
copy.
Review of *Long Drums and Cannons. Manchester Evening News*, January
16, 1969.
Review of *Long Drums and Cannons. Fiddlehead* 80 (May-June-July 1969):
105-6.
Review of *Long Drums and Cannons. University of Toronto Quarterly* 40
(Summer 1971): 359-60.
Review of *Long Drums and Cannons. Canadian Literature* 42 (Autumn
1969): 91-3.
Review of *Long Drums and Cannons. Tamarack Review* 52 (1969): 78-9.

The Fire-Dwellers

A.A.B. Review of *The Fire-Dwellers. Bristol Press* (Bristol, Conn.), June 27,
1969. Also in *Charleston New and Courier* (S.C.), June 15, 1969; *Durham
Herald* (N.C.), June 22, 1969; *Elizabeth City Advance* (N.C.), June 18,
1969; *Berkeley Gazette* (Calif.), July 5, 1969; *News-Telegram* (Sulphur
Springs, Texas), June 30, 1969; *Everett Herald* (Wash.), July 5, 1969;
Monroe News (Mich.), June 16, 1969; *Richmond Independent* (Calif.),
July 5, 1969; *Pueblo Star-Journal* (Colo.), June 22, 1969; *Las Cruces Sun
News* (N.M.), August 21, 1969; *Sunday News* (Manchester, N.H.), June
15, 1969; *Poughkeepsie Journal* (N.Y.), July 6, 1969; *North Penn Reporter*
(Lansdale, Penn.), June 5, 1969; *Californian* (Bakersfield, Calif.), June 15,
1969; *News* (Snyder, Texas), June 15, 1969.
Ballstadt, Carl. "Rachel's Ultra-Lucky Sister, Stacey, Proves She's Not So
Lucky After All." *Hamilton Spectator*, June 14, 1969.
Callaghan, Barry. "A Ladybird Lost in Limbo." *The Telegram*, May 3, 1969.
Cook, Michael. Review of *The Fire-Dwellers. Evening Telegram* (St. John's,
Nfld.), June 17, 1969.

Engel, Marion. "The girl who escaped from Manawaka is at the core of Margaret Laurence's new novel." *Saturday Night,* May 1969.

Daughtrey, Anita. "Life in a Small World." *Fresno Bee,* (Calif.), July 6, 1969.

French, William. "A Compassion for Flesh and Blood." *The Globe Magazine,* May 3, 1969.

Doyle, Clara M. Brief mention of *The Fire-Dwellers. Chronicle* (Elizabethtown, Penn.), June 12, 1969.

Grey, Bernice. "Forty-Year-Old Woman Comes to Grips with Treadmill Routine." *Beaumont Journal* (Texas), July 18, 1969.

Hayman, Ronald. Review of *The Fire-Dwellers. The Sunday Telegraph,* May 4, 1969.

Hoagland, Joan M. Review of *The Fire-Dwellers. Literary Journal,* May 1, 1969.

Hood, Stuart. "Post-Freudian, Pre-Freudian." *The Listener,* (London), May 1, 1969.

J.W. "Woman Alive." *Chatelaine* 42 (June 1969): 8.

Kattan, Naim. "Une Femme de Quarante Ans." *Le Devoir* (September 13, 1969).

King, Susan T. Review of *The Fire-Dwellers. State Port Pilot* (South Port, N.C.), July 9, 1969.

Le Butt, Paul. Review of *The Fire-Dwellers. The Daily Gleaner* (Fredericton). No date available.

Legate, David M. "She Pines Amid the Firs." *The Montreal Star,* April 16, 1969.

Lindau, Betsy. Review of *The Fire-Dwellers. Southern Pines Pilot* (N.C.), June 11, 1969.

Loercher, Diana. "'Everyday Housewife': Her Price for Coping." *Christian Science Monitor,* June 12, 1969.

Lord, Barbara. "Find or Lose." *American-Statesman* (Austin, Texas), August 24, 1969.

McGhee, Karen. "Everything will be just fine when I'm 18 again." *Book Week/Chicago Sun-Times,* May 4, 1969.

M.H.M. "Fine Novel Fashioned From Drab Materials." *Columbus Dispatch* (Ohio), July 6, 1969.

Ovedoff, Deborah. "Recognizable Woman: Fears, Joys and Ennui." *Philadelphia Bulletin,* June 22, 1969.

Petterson, Lynette. "It's all at the Y.W.C.A.: Motto for 1974." *Peterborough Examiner,* September 18, 1974.

Proctor, John. Mention of *The Fire-Dwellers. Chippewa Falls Herald-Telegram,* (Wisc.), July 5, 1969.

Riley, Mary Ann. Review of *The Fire-Dwellers. News-Advertiser* (Creston, Iowa), June 10, 1969.

Riley, Mary Ann. Review of *The Fire-Dwellers. Carroll Times-Herald* (Iowa), June 4, 1969.

Rinard, Sally. "Amours of a housewife, 40." *Wilmington News* (Del.), July 1, 1969.

Simon, Marion. "Mrs. Laurence Creates Another Vibrant Heroine." *National Observer* (Silver Springs, Md.), June 9, 1969.

Spettique, D.O. Review of *The Fire-Dwellers. Queen's Quarterly* 76 (Winter 1969): 4, 722-4.

Sullivan, Shirley K. "Reluctant Ladies." *Houston Post*, June 22, 1969.

Swayze, Walter. "The Odyssey of Margaret Laurence," *The English Quarterly* 3 (Fall 1970): 7-16.

Sykes, Philip. Review of *The Fire-Dwellers. Maclean's*, May, 1969.

Sypnowich, Peter. Review of *The Fire-Dwellers. Toronto Daily Star*, April 29, 1969.

Terrien, Margaret. "Rachel's Sister Proves Simpatico." *Independent Journal* (San Rafael, Calif.), June 28, 1969.

Thornton, Eugenia. "This Worn Theme Is A Gem." *The Plain Dealer* (Cleveland), May 11, 1969.

Tracy, Honor. "In Vancouver, Stacey found that Richalife had its drawbacks." No publication title or date.

Watt, F.W. Review of *The Fire-Dwellers. The Canadian Forum*, July, 1969.

Weeks, Edward. Review of *The Fire-Dwellers. Atlantic Monthly*, June, 1969, pp. 112-113.

White, Ruth M. "'Rachel' Author Returns." *Pittsburgh Press*, June 15, 1969.

Williams, Sally. "The Marriage Trap." *Evening Standard*, May 13, 1969.

Review of *The Fire-Dwellers. Chapel Hill Weekly* (N.C.), June 8, 1969.

Brief mention of *The Fire-Dwellers. News* (Ludington, Mich.), June 12, 1969.

Mention of *The Fire-Dwellers. Commercial Appeal* (Danville, Va.), June 9, 1969.

Mention of *The Fire-Dwellers. Huntingdon News* (Penn.), June 16, 1969.

Review of *The Fire-Dwellers. Booklist* (Chicago), June 15, 1969.

Brief mention of *The Fire-Dwellers. New Ulm Journal* (Minn.), July 17, 1969.

Draft of a six-page review of *The Fire-Dwellers*. No author, no date, no place of publication.

Review of *The Fire-Dwellers. The New Yorker*, May 31, 1969, pp. 115-6.

Review of *The Fire-Dwellers. Fort Worth Press* (Texas), June 8, 1969.

Review of *The Fire-Dwellers. Atlantic Advocate* 59 (May 1969): 56.

Review of *The Fire-Dwellers. Executive* 11 (August 1969): 56.

Review of *The Fire-Dwellers. Maclean's Magazine* 82 (June 1969): 98.

Review of *The Fire-Dwellers. Montrealer* 43 (June 1969): 9.

Review of *The Fire-Dwellers. Canadian Literature* 43 (Winter 1970): 91-2.

Review of *The Fire-Dwellers. Fiddlehead* 82 (November-December 1969): 72-3.

Review of *The Fire-Dwellers. Tamarack Review* 52 (1969): 76-7.

Review of *The Fire-Dwellers. University of Toronto Quarterly* 39 (July 1970): 344-5.

A Bird in the House

Atkins, Hal. "Rich Thoughts of Poor Era: Canada In The Depression." *Seattle Post-Intelligencer, Northwest Today*, March 29, 1970.

Baird, Dorwin and Verna. Book review of *A Bird In The House* for radio series, Book Mark, broadcast from 20 stations in B.C. and Ontario, May 1970.

Baskin, Bernard. "Laughter and Nostalgia." *Hamilton Spectator*, May 2, 1970.

Berridge, Elizabeth. Review of *A Bird In The House. Daily Telegraph*, May 21, 1970.

Bishop, Dorothy, Review of *A Bird In The House*, *Ottawa Journal*, March 28, 1970.

B.M.H. "Vivid Memories of Childhood." *Prairie Messenger*, August 20, 1970.

Boyd, John. "Old Friends." *The Irish Press* (Dublin), May 11, 1970.

Brewster, Elizabeth. "Town That's Practically Real." *The Edmonton Journal*, April 3, 1970.

Brooke Jones, Carter. "Growing Up On The Canadian Prairies." *The Evening Star*, March 2, 1970. Also in *Washington Star* (Washington, D.C.), March 2, 1970.

Callaghan, Barry. "A Cold Universe." *The Telegram* (Toronto), February 28, 1970, p. 63.

Calverley, Joan. Review of *A Bird In The House. Worcester Telegram*, March 29, 1970.

C.E.C. "The effect of a novel in eight short stories." *Montreal Gazette*, April 25, 1970.

Chubb, Dell. Review of *A Bird In The House. Post Dispatch* (St. Louis, Mo.), March 1, 1970.

Dewar, Nicole. "An All-Canadian Bird Is Captured." *Cornwall Standard-Freeholder*, March 6, 1970.

Dingman, Jocelyn. "Stories That Re-live A Familiar World." *The United Church Observer*, May 15, 1970.

Drake, Antiss. 1st proof of a review of *A Bird In The House. Book Week.* Date unknown.

French, William. "Coming of Age In Manawaka." *The Globe Magazine* (Toronto), March 14, 1970.

Gillies, Marjorie, "A Bird In The House: Good Summer Reading." *The Daily Journal Record*, May 29, 1970. Also printed in *Oakville Daily Journal*, May 14, 1970.

Harder, Helga. "For my aunts and my children." *The Canadian Mennonite* (Altona, Man.), May 15, 1970.

Hepher, Peter L. "Margaret Laurence works magic with a simple theme." *Calgary Albertan*, May 16, 1970.

Huckvale, Jane. "A Childhood Remembered." *Lethbridge Herald* (Alta.), June 13, 1970.

Ikerman, Ruth C. Review of *A Bird In The House. Los Angeles Times*, March 15, 1970.

J. M. Review of *A Bird In The House. The Evening Post and Chronicle*, Wigan, Lancashire, May 9, 1970. Also published in *Lancashire Evening Post* (Preston, Lancashire), May 9, 1970.

Kirkwood, Hilda. Review of *A Bird In The House. The Canadian Forum*, September 1970, pp. 221-222.

Legate, David M. Review of *A Bird In The House* in a Canadian tabloid (Montreal). Date Unknown.

Lister, Richard. "Vanessa through the peephole." *Evening Standard* (London), April 28, 1970.

McKenna, Isobel. "A Prairie Adolescence." *The Guardian* (Ottawa), March 25, 1970.

Malleck, Bonnie. "Dustbowl Days." *Kitchener-Waterloo Record*, June 1, 1970.

Michalopoulos, Andre. "A Trip Back In Memory." *Texas Light* (San Antonio), March 22, 1970.

Millar, Neil. "Where Hope Never Stops Hoping." *Christian Science Monitor*, March 26, 1970.

Monk, Wendy. Review of *A Bird In The House. The Birmingham Post* (Birmingham), May 2, 1970.

Murphy, Iseult. Review of *A Bird In The House. The Sunday Press* (Dublin), May 10, 1970.

Portman, Jamie. "Growing Up In Sad Times." *Herald Magazine*, May 1, 1970.

Rapoport, Janis. Rough draft of a review of *A Bird In The House.*

Saunders, Tom. "Growing up in Manawaka." *Winnipeg Free Press*, April 11, 1970, p. 21.

Scherbain, Gary. "Depressing Tales of a little Manitoba town." *The Winnipeg Tribune*, June 3, 1970.

Stafford, Ellen. Review of *A Bird In The House. Stratford Beacon-Herald* (Ont.), June 13, 1970.

Stainsby, Donald. "She Puts Life Breath Into Canadian Cliche." *Victoria Daily Times*, March 14, 1970.

Stainsby, Donald. Review of *A Bird In The House. The Vancouver Sun*, May 29, 1970.

Synpowich, Peter. "Resurrection of a Puritan." *Toronto Daily Star*, May 29, 1970.

Synpowich, Peter. "Margaret Laurence: A Puritan Girlhood." *Toronto Daily Star*, February 28, 1970, p. 69.

Thompson, Kent. "Margaret Laurence: *A Bird In The House.*" *The Fiddlehead*, 84 (March, April 1970): 108-11.

Thompson, Kent. "Margaret Laurence: *A Bird In The House.*" CBC Book Review, April 10, 1970.

Thompson, Kent. "Margaret Laurence: *A Bird In The House.*" Script.

Thompson, Kent. "Margaret Laurence: *A Bird In The House.*" CBC Book Review, Fredericton.

Thornton, Eugenia. "From Margaret Laurence." *The Plain Dealer* (Cleveland), 1970.

Walsh, Anne C. Review of *A Bird In The House. The Phoenix Gazette* (Arizona), March 7, 1970.

Ward-Harris, E.D. "Wait For 'Big One' Continues: Margaret Laurence, Canada's Literary Enigma." *The Daily Colonist*, March 29, 1970.

Wellejus, Ed. "Ordinary Events." *Times* (Erie, Penn.), March 19, 1970.

Whalon, Moira. "Compelling Biographical Short Stories." *Peterborough Examiner*, May 21, 1970.

Whately, Rosaleen. "The Patriarch In A Prairie Family." *Liverpool Daily Post*, May 13, 1970.

"Small Town In Depression Setting For Canadian Work." *Picton Gazette*, March 11, 1970.

Review of *A Bird In The House. Manchester Evening News*, April 23, 1970.

"Frustrations and Fantasies." *Time*, May 4, 1970.

Review of *A Bird In The House. Brockville Recorder and Times* (Ont.), February 27, 1970.

Review of *A Bird In The House*. American periodical. Date unknown.

"Stories Capture Mixed Emotions of Growing Up." *St. Catharine's Standard*, March 28, 1970.

Mention of *A Bird In The House* in "Books Received." *The Canadian Mennonite*, April 24, 1970.

Review of *A Bird In The House. Guardian Journal* (Nottingham), June 3, 1970.

Review of *A Bird In The House. Canadian Literature* 50 (Summer 1970): 221-2.

Review of *A Bird In The House. Liberté* 12 (juillet-août 1970): 85-7.

Review of *A Bird In The House. Saturday Night* 85 (August 1970): 26-7.

Jason's Quest

C.F.P. "Delightful Yarn." *Saskatoon Star Phoenix*, July 11, 1970.

E.D.W.-H. "What's Happened To Margaret Laurence?: Brilliant Novelist Flounders in Juvenile Field." *Daily Colonist*, September 3, 1970.

Elliott, John K. "Jason the Mole has Something for Young and Old." *The London Free Press*, June 20, 1970.

Freeman, Judi. "A Classic Tale For All Ages." *Victoria Daily Times*, July 3, 1970.

F.W.M. "Children's Allegory." *Calgary Herald*, September 1, 1970.

Goldsborough, Diana. Review of *Jason's Quest. Toronto Daily Star*, June 20, 1970.

Hay, Bryan. Review of *Jason's Quest. The Telegram*, June 22, 1970.

Johnston, Jean. "Mere Allegory." *Kitchener-Waterloo Record*, September 1, 1970.

Kapica, Jack. "Delightful Sub-Teen Book." *Montreal Gazette*, July 18, 1970.

Lunn, Janet. "Boys, seals, wolves, moles and a girl with big feet." *Globe and Mail* (Toronto), June 27, 1970, p. 17.

Preddie, Calvin. "This Book Bit Much For Kiddies." *Cornwall Standard-Freeholder*, August 4, 1970.

Reynolds, Marilynn. "An Unlikely Search Beneath Our Feet." *The Edmonton Journal*, July 3, 1970, p. 59.

Saunders, Tom. "Of Moles and Men." *Winnipeg Free Press*, July 18, 1970, p. 20.

Stainsby, Donald. Review of *Jason's Quest. The Vancouver Sun*, June 19, 1970, p. 34A.

Swan, Susan. Review of *Jason's Quest. The Telegram* (Toronto), August 8, 1970.

"New and Noteworthy" *Daily Times*, (Gloucester, Mass.), September 1, 1970.

Review of *Jason's Quest, Halifax Mail Star*, September 8, 1970.

Review of *Jason's Quest. The Kindness Club Quarterly Magazine*, September 8, 1970.

"Underground For Juveniles." *Sarnia Observer*, July 15, 1970.

Review of *Jason's Quest. Publisher's Weekly*, June 1, 1970.

Review of *Jason's Quest. Canadian Literature* 50 (Autumn 1971): 88-90.

Adilman, Sid. "Laurence novel goes over big at the libraries." *Toronto Star,* October 1, 1974.

Aiken, D.L., "Margaret Laurence Depicts The World As She Sees It." *Winnipeg Tribune,* June 22, 1974.

Bagley, Laurie. Review of *The Diviners. Georgia Straight,* June 20-27, 1974.

Barclay, Pat, "The New Margaret Laurence Novel May Redeem The Hero." *Peterborough Examiner,* May 25, 1974.

Barclay, Pat. "To Endure the Present We Must Link With Past." *Victoria Times* (B.C.), June 22, 1974.

Baskin, Bernard, " 'Diviners' taps well of freedom; work will be long remembered." *Canadian Jewish News,* June 21, 1974. Also appeared in *Hamilton Spectator,* June 1, 1974.

Biesenthal, L. Review of *The Diviners. The Canadian Reader,* 15: 5, 5-6.

Bevan, Allan. Book Review of *The Diviners. Dalhousie Review,* (Summer 1974): 360-363.

Billington, Dave, "My friend Margaret." *The Saturday Gazette* (Montreal), May 18, 1974.

Billington, Dave. Article About Margaret Laurence. *The Windsor Star,* May 25, 1974.

Billington, Dave, "*The Diviners:* a woman and her need to survive." *The Saturday Gazette* (Montreal), May 18, 1974.

Bishop, Dorothy. "Author as water witcher: a search for self." *Ottawa Journal,* May 18, 1974.

Bishop. Type-written draft of a review of *The Diviners.* July 5, 1974.

Bradford, Elizabeth, "Intimate view of an Artist in a Disappointing World." *Greensboro Daily News,* June 23, 1974.

Cameron, Donald. "The Many Lives of Margaret Laurence." *Weekend Magazine,* July 20, 1974, pp. 3-5.

Carver. Book Review of *The Diviners.* CKFM, May 19, 1974.

Cashdan, Linda. "*The Diviners* by Margaret Laurence: A Novel About Coming to Grips With One's Memories." *Books in America,* June 18, 1974.

Blackburn, Bob. Brief mention of an interview with Margaret Laurence. *Toronto Sun,* May 27, 1974.

Bresky, Louise. Review of *The Diviners.* C.B.R., Calgary, May 28, 1974.

Bruce, Phyllis. Review of *The Diviners. The Canadian Forum,* May, June, 1974.

Cameron, A. Barry. Review of *The Diviners.* Typewritten draft.

Cornborough, Julia. Review of *The Diviners. Vancouver West Ender,* August 28, 1974.

Crosby, Ann. Review of *The Diviners. The Evening Telegram,* September 28, 1974.

Doyle, Dan. "Review Criticized" (Letter criticizing a review of *The Diviners). Ottawa Citizen,* September 14, 1974.

Edgar, Luella. "A Vulgar, Obscene Childhood." *American Statesman* (Austin, Texas), September 8, 1974.

Elliott, John K. "Laurence 'Divines' Sense of Heritage." *London Free Press,* May 18, 1974.

Engel, Marion. "Margaret Laurence: Her New Book Divines Women's Truths." *Chatelaine*, May 1974.

Fulford, Robert. "Remarkable Woman." *Montreal Star*, May 18, 1974. Also in *Ottawa Citizen*, May 18, 1974.

Fulford, Robert. "Grave Lack of Readers" (Letter mentioning Margaret Laurence and *The Diviners*). *St. Catharines Standard*, September 12, 1974.

Fulford, Robert. "It's fascinating Despite the Flaws." *The Toronto Star*, May 18, 1974.

Garnet, Marion Simon. " 'The Diviners' Is A Determined Kind of Book." *The National Observer*, May 11, 1974.

Grosskurth, Phyllis, "A looser, more complex, more sexually uninhibited Laurence. And never an Atwood victim." *The Globe and Mail*, May 4, 1974.

Helwig, David. Review of *The Diviners*. *Books in Canada*, June-July 1974.

Hepher, Peter. "Everywoman, Plus the compleat Morag Gunn." *Calgary Albertan*, June 1, 1974.

Homer, Merlin. "Diviners mixes myth, intensity of feeling." *Toronto Citizen*, June 1974.

J.W.R.R. "Success to degree." *Saskatoon Star Phoenix*, May 31, 1974.

Kattan, Naim, "L'ambitieux roman de M. Laurence." *Le Devoir* (Montreal), July 27, 1974.

Kaylor, Vera. Review of *The Diviners*. *Chattanooga Times* (Tenn.), September 8, 1974.

Kiely, John. "But it's only a Canadian novel." *Kitchener-Waterloo Record*, June 22, 1974.

Kostash, Myrna. "Two Recent Canadian Novels." Miss Chatelaine, Summer, 1974, p. 12.

Lamont, Margo. Review of *The Diviners*. *The 4th Estate* (Halifax), June 13, 1974.

Lamont, Margo, *"The Diviners,"* *The Scotian Sun* (Port Hawkesbury, N.S.), June 5, 1974.

Lamont, Margo M. Typewritten copy of review of *The Diviners*, May 30, 1974.

Larkin, Joan. "Laurence of Canada." *Ms.*, November 1974, pp. 96, 100.

Leech, Maggie. "Margaret Laurence—Bowing Out." *The Columbian*, June 8, 1974.

Lever, Bernice. Review of *The Diviners*. *Canadian Author and Bookman* 50 (Fall 1974): 1, 26.

Ley, Lynette. "One for the books." *The Woodstock Bugle* (N.B.), June 26, 1974.

McCabe, Carol. "Living With Grace The Life She Has." *Providence Journal-Bulletin* (R.I.), September 8, 1974.

McDonald, Marci. "Diviners may be the last." *Star Phoenix* (Saskatoon), May 31, 1974.

McDonald, Marci. "The Author: All the hoopla gets her frazzled." *Toronto Star*, May 18, 1974.

MacSween, R.J. Review of *The Diviners*. *The Antigonish Review* 18: 107-8.

McTavish, Amelia. "What's new at the Kincardine Branch Library." *Kincardine News*, August 28, 1974.

Meuse, Alain. Review of *The Diviners*. *The Vanguard* (Yarmouth, N.S.), June 26, 1974.

Miner, Valerie. "The Matriarch of Manawaka," (Review of *The Diviners* and interview with Laurence). *Saturday Night*, May 1974, pp. 17-20.

Parks, Cameroun. "Art of water divining linked to clairvoyant powers." *Fort Wayne News-Sentinel*, September 28, 1974.

Piercy, Marge. "Gritty Places and Strong Women." *New York Times Book Review*, June 23, 1974.

P.M.B. "Margaret Laurence's Diviners—the mystic search for the wellsprings of life." *The Bracebridge Herald*, August 22, 1974.

Pratt, Martha. "Author Shows Identity of Canadian Women." *Charlottetown Guardian*, May 22, 1974.

Robb, Edith. "The Diviners." *Moncton Transcript*, May 25, 1974. Also in *Moncton Times*, May 25, 1974.

Saunders, Tom. "The Tie That Binds." *Winnipeg Free Press*, June 1, 1974.

Saunders, Tom. "If mosquitoes permit." *Winnipeg Free Press*, no date.

Silver, Kathy. Radio Review of *The Diviners*. *Radio Canada International Magazine*, June 1974.

Sinclair, Gordon. Brief mention of publicity campaign for *The Diviners*. CFRB, May 22, 1974.

Stenson, Fred, "Lavish Talent for Recreating Life." *Edmonton Journal*, June 1, 1974.

Stevens, Peter. Review of *The Diviners*. *The Windsor Star*, May 25, 1974.

Sutton, Joan. Brief Mention of *The Diviners*. *Kentville Adviser* (N.S.), August 29, 1974. Also in *Toronto Sun*, July 16, 1974.

Sweeny, Jennifer. "Two Women." *Alumni Gazette*, The University of Western Ontario, Fall 1974, p. 13.

Thompson, M.B. "Laurence's Diviners—Still 'Decently Mediocre.'" *Ottawa Citizen*, September 7, 1974.

Tulloch, Anne. "A compendium of summer reading." *The 4th Estate* (Halifax), May 30, 1974.

Unitt, Doris. "Meeting Margaret Laurence," (Interview). *Review*, October 3, 1974, p. 14.

Vickers, Reg. "Authors, gimmicks increase." *Calgary Herald*, June 20, 1974.

Walker, Elspeth. "Laurence Masterpiece." *Lethbridge Herald* (Alta.), July 27, 1974.

Weeks, Edward. "The Peripatetic Reviewer." *The Atlantic Monthly*, June 1974.

Woodcock, George. "Farewell To Manawaka?" *Vancouver Sun*, June 14, 1974.

Young, Scott. "Rewarding Reading." *The Globe and Mail*, no date.

Review of *The Diviners*. *The Province*, July 26, 1974, p. 19.

Review of *The Diviners*. *625 Insight* 3 (October 1974): 10.

Review of *The Diviners*. *The Alumni Journal*. The University of Manitoba, Winnipeg 34 (Summer 1974): 4, 18-19.

Data on Margaret Laurence. *About Books and Authors*, McClelland and Stewart, no date.

Publicity Releases on *The Diviners*. McClelland and Stewart, Toronto, 3 pgs.

Review of *The Diviners*. *St. John's News* (Nfld.), June 21, 1974.

Review of *The Diviners*. *Regina Leader Post*, June 21, 1974.

"The Diviners." *Grand Prairie Daily, Herald Tribune* (Alta.), June 21, 1974.

"Congratulations again, Margaret Laurence!" *The Victorian* (B.C.), May 29, 1974.

Review of *The Diviners*. *The Burlington Free Press*, June 20, 1974.

Review of *The Diviners*. *The New Yorker*, July 6, 1974.

Mention of *The Diviners*. *The 4th Estate* (Halifax), May 16, 1974.

"A brave and loving celebration of life." *Calgary Herald*, May 31, 1974.

Brief Review of *The Diviners*. *Calgary Albertan*, May 18, 1974.

Review of *The Diviners*. *The Publisher's Weekly*, May 1974, p. 56.

"Veteran Author: Diviners last novel." *Stratford Beacon-Herald*, July 3, 1974. Also in *The Intelligencer* (Belleville, Ont.), June 12, 1974; *Penticton Herald* (B.C.), June 7, 1974; *Sault Ste. Marie Star*, June 6, 1974; *Corner Brook Western-Star*, June 17, 1974; *Owen Sound Sun Times*, June 11, 1974; *The Chronicle-Journal* (Thunder Bay), June 4, 1974; *St. Catharines Standard*, June 1, 1974; *Evening Times Globe* (Saint John, N.B.), June 4, 1974; *Sarnia Observer*, June 4, 1974; *Guelph Mercury*, June 1, 1974; *Prince George Citizen* (B.C.), May 31, 1974; *Cambridge Daily Reporter*, June 1, 1974; *St. John's Evening Telegram*, no date available.